Face to Face

We spend years teaching our kids how to speak, when to speak, and what's appropriate to say. Once they're grown, the tables turn, and we must learn the same. In her debut book, *Face to Face: Smart Conversations with Yourself, Your Teenager, and Your Young Adult* author Patti Pilkington Reed advises parents of young adults to give our children space to grow into the beautiful human beings we've raised them to be. While being a parent is a life-long job, Reed reminds us our position is forever evolving and that while our children are growing, we must too. In *Face to Face*, Reed shares her personal experiences and offers advice to help you maintain a healthy and happy relationship with your adult child as you continue to navigate through life, together.

—**STARLENE STRINGER,**
Co-Host of *The Frank, Starlene & Hudson Morning Show*,
94.9 KLTY Radio, Dallas–Ft. Worth, TX

READ THIS BOOK! Where was *Face to Face: Smart Conversations with Yourself, Your Teenager, and Your Young Adult* when my own three passed through the "fiery furnace" from puberty into adulthood? Please do yourself a favor! Before ripping your hair out by the roots and rending your garments, glean from the wisdom of one who has "been there, done that" and then somehow survived with enough energy left in the tank to pen sound and sage advice for those who have yet to enter those turbulent waters! READ THIS BOOK! You will be so glad you did! I highly recommend it!

—**DAN DEAN,** Lead singer: Phillips, Craig, and Dean
Legacy Pastor, Heartland Church of Carrollton, TX

Navigating the years of parenting teenagers and young adults can be very challenging. In *Face to Face*, Patti Pilkington Reed provides guidance that is both inspirational and practical. Patti transparently and authentically shares from her own struggles to encourage other parents to have the courageous conversations that are necessary, and yet to learn the essential balance of knowing when to speak and when to remain quiet. This book is filled with wisdom based on biblical principles. I highly recommend it!

—**EDDY BREWER**, Ph.D., Pastor, Capital Assembly of God, Oklahoma City, OK

A place of grace...that's what we all want to create as parents...a place where we can speak with our kids' heart-to-heart and know the conversations matter. But how? Patti Pilkington Reed goes a long way in answering that question in the pages of *Face to Face: Smart Conversations with Yourself, Your Teenager, and Your Young Adult*. Her writing reflects her heart...honest and refreshing. As you walk with her through these thirty devotionals, you will learn practical ways to talk with your children about the issues that really matter...and share with them the love and grace of the one who truly matters...Jesus Christ.

—**BOB CHRISTOPHER**, President, *Basic Gospel Radio*, and author of *Simple Gospel, Simple Grace: How Your Christian Life Is Really Supposed To Work* (Harvest House).

Patti takes on parenting the teenager and young adult with effervescence and clarity. I love *Face to Face: Smart Conversations with Yourself, Your Teenager, and Your Young Adult*! I love everything about it! As a parent of a teen and young adults it was an awesome encouragement for me to read. I love Patti's heart and the help she will provide for parents. She is gifted!

—**TODD DUNN**, Pastor, 2nd Mile Church, Fort Worth, TX

Where was this book when our boys were teenagers?! Patti Pilkington Reed has crafted a beautifully compassionate and biblical guide for parents who want practical wisdom and solid support tackling the big issues with their young adult kids. The compelling way she shares her own learnings and struggles will be an invaluable support as you navigate one of the most challenging and rewarding seasons of parenting. We highly recommend this book for any parent of young adults needing direction, encouragement, and life-giving hope.

—DAVID & CARON LOVELESS,
Executive Pastor of Discipleship & Groups,
First Baptist Church Orlando, FL.
Speakers & authors of *Nothing to Prove: Find the Satisfaction & Significance You've Been Striving for at the Core of Your True Identity*

Having meaningful conversations is truly a lost art in today's culture—but Patti Pilkington Reed has accomplished writing a book which defines open dialogue and understanding the fine art of conversations, growing in trust, and creating an environment of safety! We especially recommend the questions she's written that will keep your family emotionally healthy and sustain the conversation.

—DR. GARY AND BARBARA ROSBERG,
America's Family Coaches,
Barbara Rosberg, BFA
CEO, The Rosberg Group [Authors and Speakers]

Patti draws from her personal experience and vast research, to create this engaging and practical book full of short, meaningful, biblically centric chapters focused on topics every parent struggles through. If you are looking for hope and biblical encouragement as you navigate these critical years of transition with your child, this book delivers.

—TIM FARRANT
Executive Pastor and Author
Grace Fellowship, Columbus, OH

Patti Pilkington Reed is the real treasure waiting discovery and applause in this new book. In *Face to Face*, Patti speaks to that mystifying coming-of-age narrative that blooms between parent and child, a tale best told with an adult voice. Her counsel is intelligent, and, like her English, full of light and warmth. With the authority that comes by personal experience, what she says, she says with as much optimism as grace, as much charity as precision. You will read Patti as much for Patti herself as you do for the information she delights in offering. That's her study. This is a first look.

—DAVID TEEMS,
Majestie: The King Behind The King James Bible
(Nelson/Harper Collins, 2010),
Tyndale: The Man Who Gave God An English Voice
(Nelson/Harper Collins, 2012)

Patti has raised two incredible adults, but it wasn't easy. She has had to tenaciously work to maintain a relationship with her kids, even during seasons when that was the last thing on their minds. While there isn't a foolproof formula for staying connected to your young adult children, the foundation is open communication. In *Face to Face*, Patti shows you how to keep their hearts open in some key areas where they desperately need your input, even if they don't know it yet. Any parent who wants to capture and keep the hearts of their kids who are moving toward adulthood will benefit from the wisdom found here!

—BARRETT JOHNSON,
Founder of INFO for Families
Speaker & Author of *Your Imperfect & Normal Family, The Talks,*
The Young Man's Guide To Awesomeness

The temptation when parenting teens or young adult children is to over-parent or to simply give up and walk away. Patti gives incredibly practical, biblically based wisdom on how to transition to a new, and healthy way of communicating for the next season of parenting. This book should be on every parent's reading list.

—Mario Zandstra,
President/CEO of Family Legacy, Dallas, TX

As a parent, we often have claimed God's promise in Proverbs 22:6 for our children—"train up your child in the way he should go and when he is old, he won't depart from it." It actually means to understand your child's "bent" . . . God's unique design for them... and guide them in that direction. But we soon find out this is one of the hardest tasks we will ever have as a parent.

In her wonderfully practical book, my friend Patti Pilkington Reed outlines some really unique ideas and concepts to understand your child's "bent" as this book screams out at you in every chapter saying—underline this concept, circle these words, memorize this tool!

Face to Face will help you discover new ways to connect to your child's heart. Pick it up and follow the wisdom therein!

—Joe Battaglia
Broadcaster and author of *The Politically Incorrect Jesus*
and *Make America Good Again*

Creative. Brilliant. Practical. Transformational. This book is an important framework for training next-generation leaders. The surprising twist in *Face to Face* is that, while you are learning how to have smart conversations with the teenagers and young adults in your life, you are also learning the very skills that can create smart conversations in EVERY area of your life—and theirs . . . and the results are stunning. A MUST READ for every parent who wants to connect deeply, influence deeply, and love deeply their teenagers and young adults . . . creating extraordinary relationships with extraordinary joy.

—Teena Goble
Founder/President of Transforming Talks

Face
to
Face

BROOKSTONE
PUBLISHING GROUP

The purposes of a man's heart are deep waters,
but a man of understanding draws them out.
—PROVERBS 20:5

Face
to
Face

SMART CONVERSATIONS
with **Yourself, Your Teenager,**
and **Your Young Adult**

PATTI PILKINGTON REED

Certified Coach in Conversational Intelligence®

BROOKSTONE
PUBLISHING GROUP

Face To Face:
Smart Conversations with Yourself, Your Teenager, and Your Young Adult
Copyright © 2021 by Patti Pilkington Reed

BROOKSTONE
PUBLISHING GROUP

Published by Brookstone Creative Group

Requests for information should be addressed to:
Patti Reed
P.O. BOX 651
Colleyville, Tx 76034

Unless otherwise noted, all Scripture quotations are taken from The New International Version® (NIV). Copyright © 1973, 1978, 1984, 2011 by Biblica, Inc.™ Used by permission. All rights reserved.

Scripture quotations marked ESV are taken from the ESV® Bible (The Holy Bible, English Standard Version®). Copyright © 2001 by Crossway, a publishing ministry of Good News Publishers. Used by permission. All rights reserved.

Scripture quotations marked NLT are taken from the NLT® Bible (Holy Bible, New Living Translation ©) 1996, 2004, 2007, 2013, 2015 by Tyndale House Foundation. Used by permission of Tyndale House Publishers, Inc. Used by permission. All rights reserved.

Scripture quotations marked TPT are taken from the The Passion Translation® Copyright 2017, 2018 by Passion & Fire Ministries, Inc. Used by permission. All rights reserved.

Scripture quotations marked MSG are taken from THE MESSAGE, copyright © 1993, 2002, 2018 by Eugene H. Peterson. Used by permission of Nav Press, represented by Tyndale House Publishers. All rights reserved.

ISBN: 978-1-949856-41-5 (paperback), 978-1-949856-42-2 (epub)

Cover design and Interior Layout: MelindaMartin.me

Printed in the United States of America

To Ryan Christopher and Hope Kathryn

You have taught me more than I have taught you. Thank you for the love, grace, and mercy you have extended to me over the years. Thank you for staying in the conversation with me even when it was hard. Without both of you, this book would not have been possible and for that I am grateful.

Stay connected!

Patti Pilkington Reed

Contents

FOREWORD

" I think God wants me to write a book!"

When my wife, Patti, made that exclamation to me a few years ago, it was easy for me to get on board. For twenty-nine years I have stood by her side and watched her continue to transform herself. Her background when we married was retail; she held a key buyer's position at Macy's Department Store in New York City. When we moved to Texas, she became a partner in an advertising business that she grew to a million dollars a year in sales. God led her to a miraculous exit plan that was a milestone moment in our marriage. Next, she built a direct sales business that has paid for our kids' education. I never saw that tremendous blessing coming.

In 2018, Patti became a certified coach in "Conversational Intelligence.®" C-IQ is a body of work that helps people understand what conversations open up the brain for trust, and what conversations close the brain down for distrust. Now, she has become an author and public speaker.

While I am her biggest cheerleader when it comes to business, her biggest accomplishment is Mom to our adult children, Ryan and Hope. I have watched her pray, cry, encourage, step back, step up, speak up, and shut up! That is why I am excited to write this foreword for her. The insights, wisdom, and knowledge Patti offers comes from the heart of a mom who wants nothing but God's absolute best for her kids. It's the result of a lot of trial and error, prayer, reflection, tears, resolve, and most importantly, faith.

We all have expectations of how we want the future to go for our children. But we often find that things don't necessarily go as planned or as we dreamed about. It's very much like life itself, with its hills and valleys. The key question is this: *How do you stay in a healthy and life-giving relationship with your older teen and/or adult child?* It is possible. The answer is what you will find on the pages of *Face to Face: Smart Conversations with Yourself, Your Teenager and Your Young Adult.*

—**FRANK REED**
Co-Host of *The Frank, Starlene & Hudson Morning Show*
94.9 KLTY Radio
Dallas-Ft. Worth, TX

PREFACE

A labor of love, *Face to Face* is a book birthed out of the trials, experiences, victories, hope, and everything else that accompanies the trek of parenting teenagers and young adults. In November 2017 I felt a nudge from the Lord to write. My inclination to ignore it kicked in immediately. At the time, I did not consider myself a writer. Writing never entered my mind, although I had friends who encouraged me to do so.

I began by jotting down topics that parents would consider important. I thought I could provide some possible answers and useful tools for the transitional years from childhood to young adulthood. Ideas like shifting from telling our kids what to do, to loosening the reins and giving up some control to allow space for decision-making practices made the list. A devotional format felt right.

I chose one word for each of the devotionals, like *academics, boundaries, arguments, becoming, church, conversations, anxiety* and a plethora of other important issues. Thirty hot topics came to mind. This resource supports parents in a way that allows them to exercise courage and intentionality by asking great questions of both themselves and their young adult.

Creating an environment with open dialogue and challenging questions, helps both parent and child grow in ways that will serve God and others well. These devotionals offer hope and a guide to create a life-long conversation that will take them through the seasons of life peacefully.

Being aware of our tendencies in verbiage will support the relationship's healthy evolution over time. We cannot be the same kind of mom or dad to our kids as we were when they were five, ten, or thirteen years old. Being cognizant of this is key to sustaining dialogue, in both hard and happy times. We can preserve the discussion by choosing to remain agile, flexible, and sometimes quiet. This is an acquired skill. When we choose to keep growing and allow our children to do the same, everyone benefits.

As I'm coming to the end of this project, Covid-19 surrounds us, an unexpected interruption in all of our lives. Personal, professional, and relational challenges accompany the virus. Once again, young adults are living back at home with their parents. My daughter is part of this group.

During a pandemic where we are quarantined together, what is everyone thinking and feeling? How are parents responding to their young adults and vice versa? This is a new season with no end in sight. Uncertainty abounds on many fronts. If we want to navigate this challenge lovingly and candidly, we need to practice open and honest communication about the new living arrangement.

But whether in the middle of a global pandemic or an unresolvable conflict, the pages of the Bible and this book can provide timeless and proven tools. The following devotionals offer valuable insights you can apply immediately to those relationships that mean the most to you.

My greatest aspiration is to create an environment that enables you to be courageous in discovering the God-given greatness within each of your children—and in you as a parent. I pray you develop the kind of relationship that is enduring, sustaining, and life-giving.

—PATTI PILKINGTON REED

ONE

Academics

All your children will be taught of the Lord
and great will be their peace.

—Isaiah 54:13

On a scale of one to ten, how do you and your family rate the importance of academics? How much time does your child spend engaged in schoolwork including homework each week? Do they feel pressure from school, from you, and from their peers about doing well? Would you object if they did not go to college?

Children need downtime for things they love like sports, theater, working out, hunting, fishing, video games, and more. Life cannot be all about education. As multi-dimensional individuals, we need to nurture our physical, spiritual, emotional, intellectual, and mental beings.

Consider whether or not you place an inordinate amount of pressure solely on academics. Does a focus on academics leave no room in your child's day or life for much else? Do their passions, interests, and even church go by the wayside because of too much schoolwork? Only you know that answer.

Do you dare ask your teenager/young adult how they feel about their workload at school? Do you think they will respond, "Too much work!" I challenge you to ask yourself the same question. Do you think your child's school workload requires too much work?

How does your child's schoolwork impact him in terms of rest, extracurricular activities, and friendships? Can he keep up? What about the importance of family time? How does he feel about it?

My children grew up in an affluent area that assigned a lot of weight on education. In my observation, that type of culture places the utmost importance on the *god of academics*. It seemed as though their future success required they attend college.

The push toward college, college, college can be a little nauseating. But other options do exist.

Wise parents step back and ask themselves, *Do we unconsciously give off a certain type of vibe about academics, friendships, or even church?* I am not sure we even realize what we are doing, but I do believe we send pressurized signals. And the underlying message might not be a good one, because for parents, considering another path could be scary. You may want to ask your kids if they have felt this from you—you know—*that pressuring vibe.*

Sometimes, we feel anxious about how others perceive us, if our child doesn't follow the direction most everyone else follows. But *what if*? What if they want to pursue an avenue independent from most others, and it turns out to be a tremendous learning and growth experience? Is it possible you might pressure your child to head in a direction or pathway that reflects your plan or dream and not necessarily God's?

> When we worship the *god of academics* (aware or unaware) instead of the living God, we and our children, miss out on a great adventure.

The answer to those questions is between you and God. He is a jealous God who desires a growing and intimate relationship with us and our teenager/young adult. When we worship the god of academics (aware or unaware) instead of the living God, we and our children, miss out on a great adventure.

If you relate to what I'm describing, you can change directions. God can make your crooked path, and your child's, a straight one. He is a restorative and redemptive God.

An important lesson I learned, I needed to be diligent in my prayers as I homeschooled my children (from Pre-K through seventh). It was crucial that I ask God what their education should look like for the coming year. I did my best to remain open to His leading, whether it was homeschooling, returning to private or public school, or choosing an online program. He made it clear every time. And it was different for each child.

As my children became teens, their opinions were included in the decision-making process, giving them a voice. Our discussion included their thoughts, opinions, and desires. Ultimately, Frank and I made the final decision; but we believe God led us by the Holy Spirit to the best outcomes, after we demonstrated respect to our teens.

My encouragement for you is to ASK (ask, seek, knock). Don't be afraid to ask the Lord, *What do you want for my/our child this year?* Please don't assume you know what is best. Ask the Father. Lean into Abba and listen for His answers. You just might be surprised by what you hear.

As my kids hit their teenage years, I decided not to always assume I knew what was best for them. I chose to ask Jesus if a particular choice was His best for my child. This took a certain amount of raw faith and trust on our part.

One of my children completed two years of college and decided it was not for him. He moved on to become a real estate agent. My other child had no desire to attend college. She moved to New York City at the age of eighteen to attend the acting conservatory of her dreams. These were big adjustments to the dreams my husband and I had for our kids.

We were able to make this shift because we desired God's plans for our children, not ours. He continues writing each of their stories. My version of their lives would have looked a lot different; but we chose to trust God, even when things veered from what we planned. Both of our children are figuring out their passions, and we are trusting God all along the way. We are proud of who they are becoming.

Where do academics rate in importance for you and your family? Asking God to define success in His economy may cause you to move your priorities in surprising ways. At the very least, your relationship with your child will certainly benefit from the consultation.

SMART REFLECTION

In what ways is God big enough to help your teenager/young adult figure out her path? Have you considered how you might be getting in God's way?

_____

_____

_____

_____

_____

_____

_____

_____

_____

 ## A NEW POSSIBILITY

What if you created opportunities in your child's sophomore and junior years, where she could not only visit colleges, but she could spend time with people from different industries and professions to explore all options?

Father, forgive me for not asking and for assuming what is best for my child when it comes to her education, interests, or career choices. I am open and listening quietly for Your voice. Please speak to my heart as a confirmation of the path she is to take. We trust You with our teenager/young adult's life. You know what is best.

TWO

Agreements

All you need to say is simply yes or no;
anything beyond this comes from the evil one.

—Matthew 5:37

What are some ways to navigate through the responsibilities, choices, friendships, summer jobs, or living at home again after your teen/young adult child has left the nest? Is it their first summer home after college, or are they part of the boomerang generation?

To be candid, the summer between freshmen year in college and sophomore year can be challenging. We faced obstacles with both our son and daughter during this transition. They each left home after graduating, suddenly able to make their own choices to do whatever they wanted, when they wanted. They were out from under our roof, and they were free.

Arriving back home with a few guidelines caused conflict at times. Teenagers (and humans in general) do not like to be told what to do or what not to do. It's an inner, and sometimes outward battle. All parties involved need to make adjustments to the new normal when a young adult child moves back in—even if it's only for a week.

In our case, I struggled at first with no curfews. My children adjusted to our requests to "please text me if you are not coming home." I clearly remember my frustration when I had to say, "Please do not leave your wet laundry in the washer for me to put in the dryer." And "Please do not leave your clothes in the dryer for me to fold and put away." There were a few other irritants, but you get my point.

Things change. People change and living situations change as well, even for our children. The days of angst over my children's curfews and clothes are long gone; but fortunately, we were able to come to an understanding between us. We did our best to train our children up well; but living with them as adults caused all of us annoyance at times. Thus, the need for agreements.

I hope this topic will support you in a way that will head off conflict and any challenges you may encounter. I was introduced to making agreements in order to keep the peace, whether with my children, my spouse, or even people I work with. An agreement involves everyone's input leading to a decision that is mutually agreed upon.

I believe agreements are more forgiving than mere expectations. When all parties commit, and one of the party members breaks the agreement, it then becomes about the agreement and not the person. Instead of "you let me down," or "you let us down," or "you did not keep the agreement," the focus can move toward "what we agreed to." This highlights the terms each party settled upon, instead of accusations, which raise emotions.

There is also a higher calling to agreements than to expectations. Expectations are not always discussed and most often assumed.

There is also a higher calling to agreements than to expectations. Expectations are not always discussed and most often assumed. Agreements are discussed and negotiated. There is no room for assumption when you put things in writing.

As you make agreements, you also include consequences for not keeping your side of any bargains. If the agreement is broken, there are no blow ups, no meltdowns, no screaming matches, just discussion of the things agreed upon and the consequence(s). To be clear, as Mom or Dad, it is possible that we may inappropriately breach an agreement. We have our own brokenness, and it will seep out into our children's lives. But admitting our mistakes and faults allows us to set a good example of taking responsibility.

With the help of a friend and advice from my life coach, I'm working on making agreements with my family, friends, and even co-workers. I did not practice this when my children were younger, but I make it a point to do it now.

Ideally, agreements must always begin with trust—the foundation of all our healthy relationships. If trust is not present, you will not get very far. Think of ways (ask God) how you can create a safe, loving, and open environment to come together for a discussion about whatever topic you are making an agreement about. Make sure conversations are honest and candid by all involved.

Deciding in advance how you will interact and how you will wrap up each discussion point can be valuable to the overall tone and progression of any meeting. We want to do our best to lovingly listen with an open heart, seeking first to understand before being understood. Assuming this position will go a long way in building trust that will extend into your child's young adult years.

My heart's desire is to stay in relationship with my children without compromising my values, convictions, and beliefs. I assume this is your desire too. Stay connected relationally as you enter into agreement dialogue.

Having no preconceived notions, assumptions, or judgments will go a long way in building trustworthiness. When we intentionally ask questions without an agenda and truly desire to make things work peacefully, it brings about a stronger bond. After all, our children are becoming adults. It serves them and us well if we treat them honorably.

During discussion and negotiation phases, be there to listen and ask lots of questions so you can discover what is in your child's heart. Find out what they are truly after in the agreement. Remember, the best end result or desired goal for everyone involved is peace and understanding.

SMART REFLECTION

How have you tried to make agreements in the past? How did they turn out? What could you do differently to make things work better this time around? Will you ask God?

_____

_____

_____

_____

_____

_____

_____

_____

 ## A NEW POSSIBILITY

What if you asked your teenager/young adult to experiment with you to form an agreement on a recent topic you have not been able to resolve? What if you sat down and applied some of the suggestions discussed above? What would need to change?

Lord, we have conflict at times. We struggle to come to an agreement about a variety of subjects. We ask for Your grace, peace, love, and understanding to cover over us as we try again to make an agreement that we all can feel good about.

THREE

Anxiety

Cast all your anxiety on Him because He cares for you.

—1 Peter 5:7

Have you ever received a text from your teenager/young adult saying, "Anxiety really bad this morning. Going to class late. I don't want to move"? How do we process these words when our child is away from home? The feelings associated with not being able to help or be with them are far from fun. I have wanted to pack my bag, jump in the car or plane, and go make everything better. How about you? It's hard, isn't it? I've learned to slow down in the moment, get quiet, remember the promises God has given me about my child, and text my close friends for prayer support.

When my children sent that uneasy feeling kind of text, I encouraged them to do their best to get quiet, turn on some worship music, pray, and allow God to take away the stress and anxiety. I let them know that God is always there, waiting with open arms to comfort and meet all their needs.

By grace, I've been able to choose trust in God's ability to meet my children's needs in every way. I intentionally thank Him throughout the day for making Himself known to my children. It's gotten a little easier to trust Him since I raised my kids. He is always faithful.

I've realized I must give my children the freedom to choose Jesus and press into Him. I can provide encouragement and tools, but I cannot *save* them or become their savior. Jesus does a much better job at this; and for that I am grateful.

When one of my children are distanced from me and text about their fears or anxiety, often I can only check in that evening via *Facetime*. Until then, I choose to believe he/she is learning to lean into God. He is writing a story in his/her life, and He will use it for their good and His glory. It helps me to understand that science backs up the power in faith.

I read an article recently on how anxiety, fear, and stress impact the brain. The amygdala, an almond-shaped section of the brain, is responsible for a chemical response when negative feelings occur. A simple way to combat these uncomfortable feelings such as anxiety is to breathe deep, practice meditation, and gratitude. Meditation will help calm and shrink the amygdala. Deep breathing will help get more oxygen to the brain, and gratitude will shift thoughts away from the amygdala and move us toward the prefrontal cortex. The PFC is where we can think clearly, be creative, and make good judgments about our circumstances. The amygdala lives in the back part of the brain and is activated during fight, flight, freeze, or appease moments. Slowing down and taking time to develop a consistent habit of deep breathing and meditation will improve mental health. The benefits of adopting these practices will heighten your emotional intelligence and lessen your emotional response. In other words, it instills a steadiness or calm into your reply or being. Secondly, you gain more mental clarity. Third, you become more

> Slowing down and taking time to develop a consistent habit of deep breathing and meditation will improve mental health.

self-aware, and your empathy increases. Lastly, your attention span grows giving you the ability to stay attuned and present.

God has instructed us to meditate for a very good reason, like those stated above. He nailed this anxiety thing thousands of years ago. He knows exactly what we need, when we need it; and He has provided much encouragement through the scriptures, particularly the Psalms. Find the ones that speak to your heart and pray through them, until they become part of your DNA—teach your children to do the same for their anxiousness, stress, or fear.

God desires the Word to automatically bubble up in you when anxiety rears its monstrous head. Psalm 121:1-2 says, "I look up to the mountains and hills, longing for God's help. But then I realize that our true help and protection come only from the Lord, our Creator who made the heavens and the earth" (TPT).

There are many more examples of meditation in the Bible. Genesis 24:63 says, "And Isaac went out to meditate in the field toward evening." The main reason God directs us toward meditating is to achieve perfect peace. "You will keep in perfect peace those whose minds are steadfast, because they trust in you" (Isaiah 26:3 NIV).

How do we become steadfast in our minds? We focus. We get quiet. We meditate. "Keep this book of the law always on your lips, meditate on it day and night" (Joshua 1:8 NIV).

Philippians 4:8 makes it quite clear the kinds of things we are to think about. God knows these thoughts will keep our minds in a good, clear, and life-giving place. We are to think on what is pure, lovely, and of good report. One of my favorite verses is Psalm 19:14: "May the words of my mouth and the meditation of my heart be pleasing in Your sight, oh God, my Rock and my Redeemer" (NIV).

All of these verses point us toward obtaining peace in this world. Peace from anxiety. Peace from fear. Peace from stress. God came to give us His peace. It is His gift to us. He tells us in John 14:27, "I leave the gift of peace with you; my peace. Not the kind of fragile peace given by the world, but My perfect peace. Don't yield to fear or be troubled in your hearts; instead, be courageous!" (TPT). This brings such comfort to the souls of my family, and I pray it brings just as much to yours.

SMART REFLECTION

What are you struggling with today? Fear? Anxiety? Dread? Will you ask God to pour over you (or your child) His warm and calming balm of peace? What scripture verse will you grab hold of for you or for your child?

_____

_____

_____

_____

_____

_____

_____

_____

 ## A NEW POSSIBILITY

What if you knew your teenager/young adult struggled with some hard emotions, and you asked him/her if you could take some time to pray each day? What if you asked the Lord to lift the heaviness and bring freedom to where there is bondage?

Thank You, Lord, that You have made it clear in scripture that we are to cast ALL our anxiety on You because You care for us immensely. You have also been kind enough to provide a way out of these negative and scary emotions. Please, settle my heart as You settle the heart of my teenager/young adult. I'm grateful for Your constant provision in my life. You are a good and faithful God.

FOUR

Arguments

What causes quarrels and fights among you?
Don't they come from your desires that battle within you?

—JAMES 4:1

To be completely honest, I've had lots of arguments with both my children over the years. There was the time when Ryan was in high school, I became so furious with him, I literally threw his English book out the car window. Then, there was the moment I was skiing in Colorado with my ten-year-old daughter. I completely lost my patience with her because she was not traversing the mountain like I had taught her so many years prior. She had been on skis since she was two and could maneuver well. I made a split decision to leave her. Yep, I just skied away from her and said, "Figure it out!" It was not one of my finer moments.

There were plenty of arguments that went down with my children. Feel free to ask them. They will tell you about multiple times Mama got crazy on them. Thank you, Jesus, for your forgiveness and grace.

How about you? What kinds of things have you argued about? Was it worth it? Did you find a way to resolve the disagreement, or did you sweep it under the rug to trip over it on another day? What would your teenager/young adult say about you and how you

If we can figure out the best way to clear up the struggle, we can set our kids up for success, both personally and professionally.

argue? Do you need to win? Whatever the answer, the conflict needs to be dealt with and solved for the life of the relationship. An unresolved conflict that continues to build will leave a wedge most parents would prefer to live without. If we can figure out the best way to clear up the struggle, we can set our kids up for success, both personally and professionally.

About a month ago I had a big blow up with my daughter. It wasn't pretty. I had just spent the last five days in New York City helping her get set up in her first apartment. Everything went great, until it wasn't. The morning arrived, and I was to depart later that day. However, my flight was canceled. My daughter had emotionally prepared for my leaving and would be spending the next two weeks alone. She also planned for some friends to come stay the night, and she had additional issues that were being worked through. At the time, I was unaware of these other matters. When I told her my flight canceled, she came undone. I did not understand. I thought she was completely overreacting to something I had no control over. We decided to go our own ways.

I headed toward Central Park, and she went to work. Later that evening she arrived home still upset. The reason I knew she was upset is because my daughter has the gift of reconciliation. She does not stay out of relationship with anyone for very long. She exhibits such strength, a humility when it comes to restoring conflict with the people she cares for. I love this about her. It's a gift from God. Whenever I see her exercise reconciliation, I commend her for her initiative and courage in going first. Not everyone is willing to make the first step toward restoring what is broken, but she is. One day

I believe she will be a catalyst for others to help them heal the brokenness and conflict that exist in their lives.

I wanted to reconnect with my daughter that day, and there was no way I was leaving New York with a rift between us. I needed to understand where she was coming from, what she was thinking, and how she was processing her thoughts. I was also willing to listen to her heart without judgment. That was key. That was my way "in." I knew I had to clear my own heart and mind of presumption—of any fiction I had created over the years. I wanted nothing to hinder the chance of resolving the conflict with my daughter.

I did my best to set the stage for reconciliation. I attempted to listen well, so I could first understand her thoughts and feelings, before trying to express my own. We have always taught our children about forgiveness and starting over. Matter of fact, we don't say, "I'm sorry" often. Instead, we ask, "Will you forgive me for . . . ?" Then we name the particular offense. Sometimes, "sorry" is way too easy, and asking to be forgiven for a named transgression helps clear our conscience.

To make peace with my daughter, I walked into her room with an umbrella in my hand and asked if she would stand under it with me. She laughed and said, "yes." We both laughed. The umbrella was a device, a gimmick. It wasn't raining, but with both of us under the thing it leveled the playing field. It put us on equal footing, so to speak—no longer mother to child, but friend to friend. This silly exercise demonstrated, without words, that I was willing to come close to her and see, hear, and know how the *rain* affected her.

She opened her heart. I gained new clarity and perspective of my child that day.

I also learned something about myself. It was as much an exercise for me as it was for her. I asked her questions, and I didn't assume the answers. I suppressed my need for dominance and control in deference to the bigger picture, which was reconciliation. It became more important, and necessary, to listen, to labor, and to understand my daughter without the old patterns. Understanding blossomed between us, and a new level of trust had begun. I got it.

This type of exchange demands self-sacrifice. It will mean putting the need of someone else over that of our own. But with wise, well-informed steps and proper attention to detail, it can lead to real understanding and a deepening of a relationship. Putting ourselves on a cross isn't easy. But the result? The return on your investment? New life, new possibilities, and all the old forms vanish quietly away. How about you? Do you need to have a chat with your teenager/young adult and seek to understand first before being understood? Try it and let me know how it turns out.

SMART REFLECTION

What conversation would you like to have with your child about a recent misunderstanding?

_____

_____

_____

_____

_____

_____

_____

_____

 ## A NEW POSSIBILITY

What if you just listened and asked lots of questions about the argument? What if you asked about what they really meant with certain words? Our understanding of what something means and their understanding, are most often quite different.

Lord Jesus, help us in our need. We are so quick, at times, to blame and argue because we feel hurt or disrespected. Help us to step back and take a breath and begin to ask questions like, "What is going on inside of me that I am reacting in this way? What could possibly be going on with my child?"

Help me to know when to step away, and when and if, to revisit at another time, so we don't say things we will regret later. Thank You, Lord, for Your unending grace and mercy as we grow in our relationships with those we love the most in our lives.

FIVE

Becoming

…With man this is impossible, but with God all things are possible.

—MATTHEW 19:26

We hear a lot about "becoming" these days. What comes to mind when you think about who you are becoming as your children are becoming young adults?

For me, *becoming* is about a growth mindset. Simply put, it's about adopting a viewpoint toward learning and resilience as we move through all the seasons of life. When we continue to have dreams, set goals, and have intentions about the possibilities of what could be, we position ourselves for a full life in Christ. Being purposeful to move toward spiritual growth, personal development, and the support of others will allow you to flourish in all God has created you to be. This process happens in both solitude and in community.

In my own process of becoming, I've had to slow down, particularly in this last year. Slow is not in my DNA. It actually pains me to say it because I have always been a woman of action, achievement, and results—a "hand to the plow" kind of girl.

I have an insightful and life-giving coach who has guided me for over three years. In one of our sessions, we talked about the concept of slowing down, quietness, and reflection. She asked me a question,

"Do you believe there could be multiplication (increase, compounding effect) in the slowing down process?"

At the time, it made absolutely no sense to me. We discussed the topic at length, and I agreed to experiment with the concept. As I began to adopt the practice of slowing life down, the more I saw my life begin to expand. Writing this book, opening a coaching practice, creating workshops, finding new ways to lead my network marketing team, and hosting online book studies were all little births exploding inside of me looking for expression.

As excited as I was in these new beginnings, I also struggled with my inner critic of doubt. What I found helpful was to verbalize to my coach, my friends, my husband, and even my kids what negative thoughts were hampering my actions to keep going. We all know it is a battlefield of the mind as we venture into something new, something we are creating. *Can I really do this? What will people think of me? Do I have what it takes to build a business? What will I do when my children leave home, and will we still be close? She is so much better at this than me. I can't compete with her.*

Fortunately, the gift of reflection entered my life, and I learned to overcome the critical mindset and challenges I see so many facing, including myself. With the love, support, and encouragement of my husband, friends, and team members, I moved forward. Spending time daily and extended time monthly, I thought through what God was teaching me, what I was applying, and what I could do differently to achieve my intentions.

Today, with God's help, I continue to build my businesses with a strong mental attitude. I ask myself better questions that will serve the Lord, others, and myself well. He has used all my experiences to help me grow in ways I would not have considered in the past.

When you become an empty nester or pre-empty nester, you will have more time on your hands to pursue the things, ideas, businesses, hobbies, and passions you have dreamed about. As I raised my children and homeschooled them through the seventh grade, I owned and operated my own business. I had a competent team of people who worked for me, so I could teach my children and give them the best of my day, which was important to me.

A few months after my daughter left to pursue her acting dream in New York City, the Lord began to stir my heart concerning what I love to do and what I was most passionate about. As I spent quiet, restful time with Him, here is what emerged. I focused on four things I do naturally and have a passion for: *equipping, giving, freedom,* and *family.* I am all about equipping others. I have a heart to give abundantly. I love seeing people become free from emotional bondage through spiritual principles and truths. And my family is my top priority.

I particularly love introducing spiritual and emotional freedom to others and watching them take steps toward detachment from the things that hold them back both personally and professionally. Growing up in an alcoholic home made me a candidate for all kinds of dysfunctional behavior. Most of my teenage years were spent partying with friends and staying away from home. Then there was college. I spent a year at the Fashion Institute of Technology in NYC. I learned some great things about buying and merchandising, but I decided that was not for me. I left New Jersey and headed west to California to be near my brother. At nineteen, I packed everything I owned into two bags, bought a one-way ticket, and left for a greater adventure in life. Because of that choice, I found my own personal and spiritual freedom through a relationship with

Jesus. Finding Christ enabled me to discover a trust and a love that only He can provide.

Now, I love my family and support them in the best possible way. I inquire of the Lord frequently how to love them best, so they feel accepted by me. I am grateful that I have healthy relationships with both my children. This came because of intentional and courageous conversations, deciding to listen first before sharing my perspectives, and patience with their own life journey, allowing them to figure out what was best for their lives.

Today, my heart's desire is to continue becoming an influential world changer for Jesus. I do my best to pay attention daily to the people who God puts in my path. This may be connecting someone to a small group at church, referring my hair stylist, or teaching someone how to add an additional stream of income to their budget. I may offer to mentor a young girl, ask a single mom to coffee who just moved here, or lead a young, single pregnant woman to the Lord at the New Orleans airport. Paying attention and staying aware have helped me make an impact on the world around me.

Writing this book was never on my radar; but God asked, and I said "yes." I am becoming a writer. Though my heart never entertained authorship, I am ardent about equipping others on their venture through life. Writing has been an indispensable tool. I am grateful for the experience, and I have gained so much in the process.

> Becoming is never about the destination; it is *always* about the journey.

Becoming is never about the destination; it is *always* about the journey. What about you? Who are you becoming in this season of life? Are you ready?

Smart Reflection

Who are you becoming? How are you making a difference and influencing those around you each and every day?

_____

_____

_____

_____

_____

_____

_____

_____

_____

 ## A New Possibility

What if you consciously became (with the help of the Holy Spirit) the person you have always desired to be? How would that alter your relationships, both personally and professionally? What would be the cost if you didn't choose transformation by the promptings of the Holy Spirit?

Father, because everything is possible with You, would you help me to mature into all You see me to be. In Jesus' name.

SIX

Birthing

My dear children for whom I am AGAIN in the pains of childbirth until Christ is formed in you.

—GALATIANS 4:19

How are you handling your child's transition to young adult? Is it what you thought it would be or does it look different than you were hoping?

My life changed in radical ways when God placed Ryan Christopher and Hope Kathryn into my arms and into my care. I did not realize then how these two little packages of love would impact my life beyond what I could have imagined. They have contributed in a significant way to the mom, wife, and woman I am today.

My children's influence on me was possible because I let them into my heart and my soul. I allowed them to respectfully speak into my life and call me out when needed. I admit, it hurt at times, but it also alerted me to my own brokenness and produced a humble spirit of repentance before them. I let my children open their hearts to me without judgment. I also let them see my joy and my delight in the ways God was teaching me new things each day.

I did a better job being vulnerable with my daughter than I did with my son. This has caused some regret for me. But I also know

God's constant presence of grace and love, even with my parenting flaws. I have asked both my children on different occasions, "Do you see how much I need Jesus too?" It was important for them to know I was still in need of God's kindness to move me forward in my own maturity.

I am grateful God gave me the wisdom and grace not to hide my sinfulness from my children or others; but instead, has encouraged me to be an open book (at the appropriate time). Letting others into my world, allows them to see my great need for Him. In our vulnerability, we allow the Holy Spirit to use us to support others in their own time of healing.

How about you? Have you let your young adults in? Have they ever seen your brokenness?

> In our vulnerability, we allow the Holy Spirit to use us to support others in their own time of healing.

Just as Christ is being formed in us, He is forming Himself in our children. Just as transformation is a slow process in our lives it can be gradual in theirs too. I watch my kids wrestle and struggle in their faith and beliefs while I wait for Christ to form Himself in them. To be honest, it's been tough; and I've wanted to scream at times, as I poured my life strength into exposing my children to a living, breathing relationship with Christ.

I have learned to refrain on more than one occasion from saying things that would most likely offend them or that they are not ready to receive from me. I've heard that still, quiet voice inside me say, "Not now, Patti." For those who know me, holding my tongue is not my forte.

I am happy to report that I am growing, learning, and getting better in this area. Being quiet about my opinions or the truth in

God's Word takes Holy Spirit wisdom and restraint. My children know the truth I poured into them for eighteen years. I've decided and chosen to listen carefully, to encourage them greatly, to be there when I can, to not offer advice unless asked, to refrain from always having an answer, and to allow them to do battle with the testings of life. I believe releasing my children and letting God do His work in and through them will bring about God's birthing process of faith, not mine.

When we force or demand them to grow in their faith, it will most likely backfire. As we acquiesce and allow God to write our children's stories He will weave together the tapestry of their lives. God's faithfulness will ultimately form the love, life, and character of Jesus Christ within them.

Will you take courage, be brave, and let Jesus birth His life of faith in your children? The process won't look like you would expect it to. Or maybe it will. It hasn't for us. But the outcome is worth any concern you may hold. I encourage you to let Him have His way with your most precious gifts.

SMART REFLECTION

What area in your life would you like to be vulnerable about with your young adult? How could that help him? And you? How has he seen your brokenness, your pain or hurt? Does she know you need Jesus just as much as she does?

_____

_____

_____

_____

_____

_____

 ## A NEW POSSIBILITY

What if you created an occasion to be open, honest, and transparent (by the prompting and guidance of the Holy Spirit) to have a heart-to-heart about the results of your own woundedness. Maybe you could tell your story of choosing to become better, instead of bitter about a particular area of struggle in your life. How would that feel for you, and how might it benefit them?

Father, You are kind, gentle, and patient with us as we change and mature. I pray my children would sense Your Holy Spirit working in me, and that would inspire him to walk closely with You. Physical birth is not easy, and waiting on my young adult's spiritual birth and growth might be equally as difficult. Would You grant me unconditional love, peace, and trust in You, as I wait and watch Jesus being formed in and through him? Thank You, Father.

SEVEN

Boundaries

*Everything is permissible for me, but not everything is beneficial.
Everything is permissible for me,
but I will not be mastered by anything.*

—1 Corinthians 6:12

In what ways are you looking for opportunities to help your teenager/young adult set up boundaries in their life? Are boundaries necessary, and are they even biblical?

When I think about boundaries, I think about some kind of dividing line or invisible space that exists between me and another person. I remember the time my husband and I were in counseling seeking wisdom on how to handle a particular situation with one of my young adult children. Our counselor gave a great example about boundaries and how they work best.

He said, "Patti and Frank, your home is like a tennis court. There's a net and a line around the court. Your adult children are outside the line.

"This is your game. You get to decide the guidelines for the game. Frank, you and Patti have a net between you, but you are on the court playing the game together. Your children get to decide if they want in on the game with your set of ground rules. They don't really get to call the shots. It is your home. They are welcome to play the game for as long as you'd like them to be there, but they have the choice of playing or not. They decide. Their choice. Your guidelines."

This brilliant visual gave a lot of clarity to healthy boundaries for the new season we had entered. When we model what strong and life-affirming boundaries look like at home, we can then set up our young adults to establish clear lines as they go out into the world. I had a conversation with my daughter today about someone she was working for. Her employer clearly had no boundaries on what was appropriate to say via text or in person.

> When we model what strong and life-affirming boundaries look like at home, we can then set up our young adults to establish clear lines as they go out into the world.

It was discouraging and frustrating for Hope to be approached unprofessionally and disrespectfully. The positive outcome was my daughter's ability to spot dysfunction, unhealthy boundaries, and another person's lack of emotional health. She does her best to stay clear of it. However, in work or personal relationships, it can sometimes pose a challenge to navigate.

Taking responsibility for our lives and the choices we make puts us in the proper mindset. Boundaries are in place to keep us from things that could harm us. God tells us clearly that everything is permissible, but not everything is beneficial. Everything is permissible, but we are not to be mastered by anything. Boundaries (and the help of the Holy Spirit) keep us on the path that leads to the life we were made for.

No boundaries result in destructive pathways that lead to death: emotional, mental, relational, professional, financial, spiritual, or even physical death. If you are like me, in my younger years, I made some not-so-great choices. There were consequences for those poor decisions. But by God's grace, He picked me up, restored my life, and sent me out to start fresh. My new life in Christ had boundaries which kept me secure. God tends to us and provides boundaries as a means to shelter us from the elements of life. His borders, for our lives, fall in pleasant places.

When my kids were younger, I warned them about harmful lures that were going to come knocking at their door. I said to them, "It's not if, but when you are confronted with temptation ranging from drugs, pornography, alcohol, sex, sexual preference, self-harm, gambling, excessive gaming, and a myriad of other life-negating traps, how will you respond?" I wanted them to think about what they would choose and why, when that moment of enticement struck.

Your teens will be confronted with most everything on the above list. I encouraged my kids to know how to behave and reply in advance, so they did not need to think or decide in the moment. In doing so, they were ready and kept safe.

Our kids are not going to get this one hundred percent right. My children did not in their younger years, and they are still navigating through the demands of the culture to conform to the ways of the world, while becoming who they were created to be. By the grace of God, I remain anchored in a relationship with them. I am staying in the conversation and listening to understand them first, before repeating the Word of God to them for the umpteenth time. I've learned to use discernment in the timing of what to say, how to say it, and when is it appropriate, so they will receive my counsel.

As we stay present and attentive with our children (mine have both left the nest), we listen without judging or assuming what is on their minds. We pray they will figure out how to set boundaries in all areas of their lives: relationally, physically, emotionally, financially, and professionally. In doing so, they can keep blossoming in every way and become life-giving, responsible adults who love God, themselves, and serve others in the greatest and most impactful way.

Smart Reflection

Who are you without boundaries in your life? What are some examples to chat with your teenager and young adult about, concerning how boundaries made a difference in your teen years or in your present life?

_____

_____

_____

_____

_____

_____

_____

_____

 ## A New Possibility

What if you took some time to think about the best avenue to enter into a dialogue with your child to help her establish boundaries and to stay free from what the world has to offer?

Lord, it is only by Your grace, and Your help that we can live out what You have called us to be and do. Help me model good and healthy boundaries to my teenager/young adult, so she will learn and desire to set her own. Give me courage and opportunity to share my experience with boundaries and to help her create hers. Thank You, Lord!

EIGHT

Church

Let us not give up meeting together,
as some are in the habit of doing, But let us encourage one another—
and all the more as you see the Day approaching.

—Hebrews 10:25

What are your beliefs and values about the importance of being part of a local church? What kinds of stories have you told yourself regarding your young adult children and their weekly church attendance? What if he/she says he/she is going to church, but he/she is not? What if you have young adults that have come back home? Are they required to attend with you? These are great questions to ruminate over. Our kids will not walk a straight path; none of us do. But we can entrust them to God and be confident He is watching over them.

When our teenagers leave the nest, we hope and pray they will continue down the same spiritual path of beliefs they were raised with as children. But they may not. How will you respond to them if they choose to put church on hold or decide it is not for them? It's important for us to tread lightly in this area. We don't want to push them farther away. Asking the Lord to guide us to know how to enter a conversation and what specific questions to ask will do wonders for the relationship.

We can take steps to explore and discover what is going on in our children's minds. Whatever is ruling their hearts will most likely show up in their behavior. Once we discover our child's thoughts and feelings, we better know how to pray for them, so they can recognize God's movement in their lives.

This past year, my daughter moved fifteen hundred miles away to another part of the country. Leaving her was difficult on many levels. Getting connected to a church family and finding community with other believers was a challenge. The transition into college life and getting out on her own was rocky. Add to that, past church hurts and feelings of anxiety about new surroundings, and it caused some angst.

My daughter came home for the summer after her first year at school. We had many chats about all that she was learning and discovering. One discussion in particular occurred after a church service.

She said, "What did you think about the sermon?"

I shared my response, and she said she felt the same. Then, she handed me her sermon notes to read. In addition to reviewing her comments, I enjoyed hearing her process her thoughts out loud.

The conversation helped validate my daughter's feelings and affirmed some of her doctrinal beliefs not related to salvation. Hope is quite discerning. Our conversation gave her freedom to feel differently than what was being taught that morning. She discovered she was free to process her values and beliefs on a myriad of topics in scripture, because every passage is not all fixed and one-dimensional.

My daughter sensed the freedom I was giving her, and she was able to express herself openly, honestly, and candidly. At one point in the conversation, I felt prompted by the Holy Spirit to say to her, "You are free to not go to church, but promise me you will read the

Bible. I trust you, Hope; but more importantly, I trust our big God to capture your heart. When you listen, He will speak to you in ways He knows you will hear and receive."

I couldn't believe this came out of my mouth. What in the world had I just said? But I knew it was God's Spirit impressing this upon my heart and mind.

My nineteen-year-old daughter told me the next day, "You have no idea what it means to me that you gave me that kind of freedom to choose."

Before I'd said anything, I sensed in my spirit that Hope needed freedom, but she did not want to ask for it. But were her choices to attend or not attend church for me to decide? I thank God for leading and guiding me to say what I said at the right and appropriate time.

> We are not able to give openness, love, and space to someone unless we possess that same liberty ourselves.

We are not able to give openness, love, and space to someone unless we possess that same liberty ourselves. God has set me free, and He can set you free, too. Ask Him. When we create a venue for others called choice, particularly with our children, they can feel it, sense it, and will blossom under it. What an appealing gift to give not only to your children, but to others.

Am I crazy for saying you don't have to go to church? Maybe, but I choose to pray and trust the Lord to lead my children and guide them right into His presence at any place and at any time.

In the waiting, we can stand by our children and pray until they find their freedom in Christ through a relationship that is solid in their hearts and sound in their minds. Forcing, persuading, and advocating for my children to do everything just like I did in my connection with the Lord does not work. We must give them a listening ear and room to question what they believe and why. This,

I believe, will help them create a solid faith and foundation for life. It will also empower them as responsible and gracious people to do the same for others.

Having said that, I believe whole-heartedly that the best place for young adults is to be surrounded by a community of gracious, Jesus-loving people. We are not meant to live out this life alone. Growth comes from being engaged with people. We need each other. Our young adults need the same support. However, they will need to choose for themselves. Commitment to community will not come from "you must" or "you have to" or "we expect you to." It will come from the freedom to decide how much they value their faith and the practices they have been taught while growing up. I hope and pray you will extend these liberties to your children, so they, too, will be the light and hope of the next generation of Christ-followers.

Smart Reflection

Once your young adults have left home, what kinds of choices will they have regarding church attendance?

_____

_____

_____

_____

_____

_____

_____

_____

_____

 ## A New Possibility

What if you set them free to figure things out on their own, knowing all along that God has got them?

Father, encircle my children with Your favor. Help them to recognize Your love. I pray You would consistently bring Jesus-loving people into their lives to help them, love them, and teach them about You. Show them the importance of fellowship and surrounding themselves with faith-filled people. I choose to believe You are still working even when things seem quiet.

NINE

Conversations

Let your conversations always be full of grace, seasoned with salt,
so that you may know how to answer everyone.

— Colossians 4:6

It comforts me to know God knows my heart. My words may not always convey what I'd like to say, but He knows what my intentions are. He also knows the thoughts and motives of my teenager/young adult much better than I do. God's heart for relationship is greater than we can imagine.

In days like these, competing against a phone your child looks down at every sixty seconds makes real conversation challenging. I admit I have had the same issue at times. Engaging with teenagers/ young adults for any length of time for more than five minutes is a win. I learned the hard way that the thoughts, attitudes, and words I speak have consequences on what I say to my kids. With my young adults, my heart desperately wants to stay in touch with theirs. Sometimes I do this well and sometimes not so much.

As I met with my coach this past week, we discussed how important the following four questions are in any conversation.

- *What am I thinking and feeling going into this conversation?*
- *What is my attitude?*

- *What words do I consistently use that make them no longer hear me?*

- *Am I considering the outcome that my words may have on my children?*

We usually have great intentions, but sometimes the results of those intentions look different than what we had in mind. I have experienced this with my children on more than one occasion.

In *Conversational Intelligence*®, author Judith E. Glaser says, "According to research, nine out of ten conversations miss the mark. There is now scientific research and data available on the chemical reactions and responses that occur as we interact with others through conversation. These new advances in neuroscience are giving us the tools to look inside our brains as we have conversations to reveal just what is going on and why."[1]

This information supports grabbing the opportunity to impact our relationships in the most loving and trusting way. Consider pausing, reflecting, and praying through how you want to be present in the moment and be their biggest cheerleader. Establishing a conversational ritual with your teenager/young adult during those more difficult talks is helpful.

Discuss how you can come to the conversation with some guidelines that will help make your talk a productive one, especially for those important discussions. For example, "We will always respect one another. We will not raise our voices. We will give feedback in a loving way. We will always affirm each other. We have permission to step away if needed. We will always pray at the end."

Prior to getting together, I found it helpful to take time to think about how much I love my child and why. I understand it might

---

1 *Conversational Intelligence*, Routledge Publishing, 2016

not be easy at the time to do this. Sometimes we don't like our children very much, but we always love them. Having a few questions ready to discover what is on their heart will help move things along. I suggest open-ended questions: *Tell me how. What do you mean? Help me understand.* And *what else?*

Prepare to come into the meeting without preconceived notions, assumptions, or judgments about what you think they are going to say or not say. Do your best to come in neutral. All ears. Your child will most likely check out and shut down if they sense any judgment or criticism on your part. If this is the case, you will get nowhere. Be open. Listen to understand first; then you can make your case for being understood. We are the adults in the room, and it is in our best interest and theirs to practice how healthy relationships behave.

> Prepare to come into the meeting without preconceived notions, assumptions, or judgments about what you think they are going to say or not say.

If you are not sure what your child is saying, ask them to elaborate and explain further. One word's definition to them could be interpreted completely differently for you. We assume we know and understand someone's meaning, but we know and understand from *our* viewpoint, not theirs. We all see the world differently, through our own narrow lens, filter, and history.

Do your best to comprehend from your child's viewpoint. Have some self-awareness. Check your tone, body language, facial expressions, and the words you use. Start there, and be satisfied with even a little progress. Your kids will sense a change in you, and that could make all the difference in your relationship.

Just yesterday, my girl called to talk to me about her boyfriend and their current struggle. First, let me say, *Thank you, God, that she is asking for my advice.* During the conversation, I stayed open and honest. (I was actually feeling more empathetic toward the young man's position than hers.)

I gave her my thoughts, my opinion, and told her I would pray for her about her decisions. I would not tell her what to do—she would choose. I encouraged her in her decision-making abilities. The silver lining in the conversation came when I heard her beliefs, opinions, and thoughts about her other friendships. I got a glimpse into her heart, her values, and her confidence as a young woman. Always look for the silver lining in your conversations with your kids, you will find treasures of golden nuggets hidden in between the highs and lows of the exchange. What a gift it can be!

SMART REFLECTION

What kinds of adjustments will you make to create a safe space for your child to open up and be transparent with you?

_____

_____

_____

_____

_____

_____

_____

_____

 ## A NEW POSSIBILITY

What would it look like to put your phones away and focus attention on each other? What if you had a conversation where your child felt no pressure, no guilt, or no shame. What if he was brave enough to tell you what is really on his heart?

Lord, my chats with my child are not going so well. I want to confess my role in that. Help me to change. Show me where I need to adjust. Help me to apply new ways of conversing, so we can have a strong, lasting and loving relationship, both now and in the years to come. Thank You, God.

TEN

Decisions

*Trust in the Lord with all your heart and lean not
on your own understanding; in all your ways acknowledge Him,
and He will make your paths straight.*

—PROVERBS 3:5-6

What do you do when your teenager/young adult makes decisions you don't agree with? How do you handle the possible disappointment it may bring? Will you try to force them to do something at eighteen, nineteen, or twenty years old, or will you let them choose?

There are decisions your child will consider.

- *Which friends do I hang out with?*

- *Do I want to attend church?*

- *What do I really believe about God?*

- *Which college is best for me?*

- *Why do I have to serve at church?*

- *Should I go out and party with those friends?*

- *Should I get a job?*

Having walked through a variety of these situations with our young adults, we struggled at times with making them do what we thought was best or letting them choose. I realized the day was quickly approaching when I would not be there, and they would decide for themselves on a variety of topics. Letting them choose felt like complete loss of control; but *making them* do something we thought was best, felt controlling and painful.

Last year, my daughter made a commitment to work as a camp counselor. We were very excited about the chance she was given to be a part of a thriving group of leaders. However, as the time approached, she became anxious about her earlier decision and felt in her heart she could not fulfill her obligation for legitimate reasons. At first, I did not understand, and I was frustrated and sad that she would not experience what I thought could be some life-changing moments that summer. Through prayer and discussions with my husband, we decided to let her make the choice. This was not easy. We knew people who would be disappointed. She elected to decline the opportunity.

> Giving our children unconditional love, especially when we don't agree with them, is possible only by the grace of God.

In our home, we do our best to provide open, honest, and authentic feedback about our thoughts and feelings. We let our children know when we don't agree with their decision, but we make sure they know that we love them regardless. Giving our children unconditional love, especially when we don't agree with them, is possible only by the grace of God.

It is so important to begin the process of empowering kids in their decision-making abilities in the teen years. Do not decide everything for them. Let them feel the weight, responsibility, and privilege of choosing. The consequences of those choices will follow, and hopefully will be their best teacher. I realize this is not easy, but it is very much necessary for their growth and development into responsible young adults.

I remember a time when my son was around sixteen or seventeen, and he asked if he could go camping with his friend at the local lake. I thought to myself, *It's February; it is going to be cold tonight, and there could be creepy people and wild animals walking around out there.* I am a city girl at heart, and I find the lights, people, and bustle safer. I wanted to intervene and say to my child, "No way!"

Sixteen and seventeen are the beginning of transitional times. I knew our son would leave for college in a couple of years and would then make all kinds of decisions—some good and others maybe not so good. So, in this instance, I gave him the choice and let him decide for himself. I think he may have been stunned by my response. He was expecting, "No, you cannot go."

I wanted to say, "That is an unwise decision considering the weather and all the things that could go wrong." Instead, I offered him some advice to reflect on and told him, "You decide." Then I ran to my closet and prayed.

By the end of the day, my son came to me and said, "Mom, I've decided not to go."

You can imagine my response. I said very calmly, "I think that is a very wise decision, Ryan." On the inside I was jumping up and down, knowing I would get a good night's sleep.

Can we let go of control and let God have His way with our children? Can we do this when we feel they are not making the best choice? For me, I see God weaving our children's stories together. We all know what a tapestry looks like on the reverse side. It's a messy group of tangled threads tied randomly together. It is the same with us—we are chaotic, broken, and erratic at times. As we choose to trust and lean into our Heavenly Father, we can stand confident in His presence, love, and guidance in our lives and in the lives of our children.

I was at my church yesterday, for Serve Day, and sitting at the table near the coffee shop were a few parents of young adults. I heard one father say, "I have a twenty-year-old, and it is terrifying!"

I chuckled to myself. *Yes, it is,* I thought. All the more reason to sit quietly at the feet of Jesus daily. How do we navigate these teenage and young adult years without Him? I would not recommend doing so.

When we become anxious and struggle about the decisions our kids will make or are making, I am confident of this, God will speak to you through His Word, through the encouragement of a friend, or maybe even a song on the radio. Ask God to give you wisdom, so you can steer the relationship with your child in a healthy, loving, and life-giving way. I'm certain He will not disappoint you. Your Father will help you make the right choices about your child and, when they ask; He will be there for them too.

SMART REFLECTION

What does your decision-making process involve? What kinds of experiences can you tell your children about? How has the Lord given you wisdom in the midst of making choices? "For the Lord gives wisdom; from His mouth comes knowledge and understanding" (Proverbs 2:6).

_____

_____

_____

_____

_____

_____

_____

_____

 ## A NEW POSSIBILITY

What if you sat down with your children, took out a piece of paper, and taught your young adults the skills necessary to make good decisions in the days and years ahead. What would you tell them? What are the most important points to teach them?

Father, give me wisdom to know exactly how You want me to instruct my kids when it comes to making great decisions in life. What do You want me to teach them?

ELEVEN

Expectations

...whatever you do, do it all to the glory of God!

1 CORINTHIANS 10:31

I had a fabulous conversation with my daughter centered around the topic of expectations, obligations, guilt, and truthfulness. We talked a lot about growing up in the church, how that affected her, what her true feelings were concerning her faith, and how that translated into her everyday life now that she was out on her own.

For children who grew up in the church, each of their experiences were likely different. I imagine some were good and maybe some were not so good or a mix of both. I was not raised in an evangelical environment; so growing up was a completely different experience for my kids than it was for me. They have told me so on many occasions. My children endured the additional pressure of having a father who was a public figure in Christian media. They kept their noses clean for the most part but were not perfect. It is funny how you can grow up in the same house, but have different experiences, thoughts, and feelings toward various situations. My children certainly did.

I remember a recent discussion with Hope, when I visited her in New York City. We had a fun time shopping, painting, cooking for her friends, and visiting a new church that was just a short train ride away from her apartment. We headed out Sunday morning, jumped on a subway, grabbed a coffee, and arrived at church just in time. It was a small church compared to the church she was raised in, but welcoming and warm with great worship and teaching. We enjoyed it.

Later that day, while food shopping, we had an interesting discussion about the church service, next to the chicken counter. Hope said she really liked it and would like to go back to the church, but asked herself this question, *Would I return for my parents or for me?*

Hope decided, *I will go back for me.*

Of course, my heart leapt. Every Jesus-loving parent wants to hear these words.

As much as my heart's desire is for my children to have a growing and living relationship with Jesus, I know I cannot make them, persuade them, or force them. This must come from the breath of the Holy Spirit.

If we coerce commitment, it will not be genuine on their part and will cause resentment, anger, and distance in the long run. Giving them space and time, just like God gives us space and time, may be just what they need. Quite often, we expect (and desire) our kids to continue down the same spiritual road the family has always traveled; and when they don't, it is upsetting and frustrating. I get it. I've been there. However, thinking through the best way to continue engagement with our children is wise. My answer would be this: Love. Space. Prayer. Encouragement. Acceptance. Intentionally adopting all of these actions will make a difference with your loved one, more than trying pressure or guilt tactics.

> Giving them space and time, just like God gives us space and time, may be just what they need.

I have often thought about how millennials are leaving the church in droves. *Why is that? What are they thinking? What has caused them to leave, and how can we help bring them back to an intimate relationship with Jesus and fellowship with gracious believers?*

I'm not sure formal church, as we know it, is the answer for younger generations. But bringing them back into fellowship is the heart of our Father. Fellowshipping with other believers, possibly with welcoming home churches or smaller group gatherings, might help draw them.

A lot of home churches seem to be popping up for young adults. This makes me wonder, *What is it about the **formal** church that repels them?*

For whatever reason, church, as they know it, or as it is today, may be the reason young people are leaving Christian fellowship. Honestly, I don't know the answer to keep them engaged in growing their faith; but I am making efforts to figure that out by looking for opportunities to ask lots of questions. I'm inquiring about the experiences these young adults had while growing up in Christian homes and church.

Were there rules and regulations around their faith? Did they understand the difference between the grace of God compared to the law of God? Did they ever feel they just couldn't *cut it* as a Christian? As young adults, were they given the freedom to choose once they left for college or after graduating high school? All of these questions are worth exploring with your child, if they have already left your home or they are about to leave.

Opening up a conversation around these queries may provide the key to unlocking where children are at in their walk with the Lord. Leave judgment out of your response. Do your very best to be attentive and discern what they are sharing. Let them feel they have been heard. Being empathetic toward someone and listening to their opinions will go a lot further than giving them a Bible verse (unless God is prompting you, of course). Asking them for the twentieth time if they'd like to come to church on Sunday rarely gets results. Give it a rest. Let the Holy Spirit do His work. Keep praying until the child's heart opens.

About five years ago, God gave me a verse concerning one of my children. "God will fight the battle for you. And you? You keep your mouths shut!" (Exodus 14:14 TPT). Ouch. What it comes down to is this—it is an encounter with the Holy Spirit that will move a teen/young adult back to the heart of God. When we pray and allow the Holy Spirit to have His way with us, we can be confident He will do the same for our children. He is faithful. Always.

Smart Reflection

How are you doing in the arena of keeping your mouth closed? Are you allowing the Holy Spirit to speak into your life and the life of your children? What has He said to you lately? Are you obeying?

_____

_____

_____

_____

_____

_____

_____

_____

 ## A New Possibility

What if you practiced the above and your children saw a difference? What if they began to feel more trusting with sharing their innermost thoughts and feelings? How would that change the relationship for the better?

Lord, thank You for the grace You extend to me when I mess up and don't always get it right. Thank you for stretching out the same hand of love to my children. Allow me to be an extension of You so they come to understand Your great love, grace, and the plans You have for them.

TWELVE

Failure

. . . for though a righteous man falls seven times, he rises again,
but the wicked are brought down by calamity.

—PROVERBS 24:16

We are walking through a series at my church called "Who Am I?" This past week we landed on "Who am I when I fail?" The first thing that came to mind was how I define failure. How does the world define failure? And, more importantly, how does God define failure?

As I have walked closer with Jesus and grown in my faith, my understanding of failure has changed. I believe you either succeed or you learn. Reading through many of the scriptures, the compassion of God is evident. When we fall down or might consider something a failure, He picks us up. He encourages us. He doesn't give us some negative kind of browbeating because we didn't hit the target. From what I can see, it's the opposite. His gracious, kind, forgiving, and unconditional love is always present to nourish our spirits and lead us back to Him. One of my favorite verses is Romans 2:4: "It is His kindness that leads us to repentance."

> His gracious, kind, forgiving, and unconditional love is always present to nourish our spirits and lead us back to Him.

The world's view of failure attacks the soul. It discourages our hearts. When we listen to culture, we conjure up all kinds of thoughts that do not serve God, us, or others well. To follow the world and its definition of both success and failure would be to shortchange ourselves in knowing how God views us when we do fall short. Consider the following, and grab hold of the message.

> I'm not saying that I have this all together, that I have it made. But I am well on my way, reaching out for Christ, who has so wondrously reached out for me. Friends don't get me wrong: By no means do I count myself an expert in all of this, but I've got my eye on the goal, where God is beckoning us onward—to Jesus. I'm off and running, and I'm not turning back.

—PHILIPPIANS 3:12-14 (TPT)

Or you could choose Psalm 145:3, which says, "God gives a hand to those down on their luck, gives a fresh start to those ready to quit" (*The Passion Translation*). I am all about a fresh start.

God knows both my children have given me the opportunity to pause and reflect on the concept of failure. It is not easy parenting teens and young adults these days, but it is equally difficult to stand in their shoes. My own children's mistakes have pushed me to pray more diligently and landed me on my face before God on more than one occasion. What I have come to accept and learn in moments of failure, on my part and my children's, is that *pain is grace*. Pain alerts us to what's really going on inside our hearts and helps us to recalibrate our souls to what is most important.

Have you thought about how much *stock* you're putting in your children's accomplishments, academically and athletically, or even spiritually? Are you hijacking your identity, attaching it to Johnny who has a 4.0 GPA and made the select soccer team, or to Susie, who is the lead dancer at her recital and was elected class president?

All of these things are wonderful, but what happens when they mess up or fail? Do you freak out on them or take a step back in the relationship? Do you ignore the failure and put your head in the sand? Do you pass the buck to your spouse and do nothing? I've seen all of the above; but I would say this, God is for the relationship. No matter the mistakes made, He is lovingly guiding our teens/young adults and us through these tough transitional years.

Let's be honest, our children will most likely not make it through their teenager/young adult journey unscathed. Growing up does not occur in a straight line. Kids will mess up and hopefully "fess" up because of the trust you have established in your relationship over the years. Decide in advance how you will respond to their mistakes and failures.

We are somewhat of a public family here in the Dallas–Fort Worth area. Our kids knew whose family they were a part of and did their best to honor us with their choices. But they also made mistakes. Dealing with mess ups wasn't my favorite part of parenting. We didn't always handle it in the most loving and gracious way. But God is a God of second, third, and fourth chances. We always had the opportunity to embrace the child, forgive the errors, and choose love. In doing this with our children, the relationship grew, and we developed a deeper bond. Forgiveness + love = long-term relationship.

As much as it pained me at times to hear about my children's failures, talking and working through them was the very thing that made our relationship stronger. The fact that they were willing to confide in me was a gift, and I felt privileged.

We are all broken people in desperate need of love, acceptance, forgiveness, and grace. My children know truth in their inner parts. They know right from wrong. When they make decisions that don't line up with that truth, I then have a choice—my preferred option is to forgive, love, and help direct them through the consequences of their choices. I also know how to truly pray for them.

Sometimes it is a painful gift to know the truth about our kids, but it can bring about a new freedom in the relationship, as we continually entrust them to their Creator. Deciding to engage and be present for your children when they fail is grace—grace at its best—the same grace we receive from God. My prayer is that you are able to extend the limitless love of God to each and every mistake or failure your children make as they move into and through adulthood.

SMART REFLECTION

What is triggered inside of you when your teenager or young adult fails? I'd like for you to consider asking Jesus these questions: How do my teenagers' and young adults' mistakes and failures affect me as a parent? In what ways do I base my identity and worth on my children's successes, failures, good grades, rank in their class, or what college they may be attending, their status and achievement as an athlete, and so on?

_____

_____

_____

_____

_____

_____

_____

 ## A NEW POSSIBILITY

What if you set aside a time with no distractions, a secure and trusting place for your children to process the issues of life? What would that look like? How would that feel? What if you taught them this: We either win or learn? What if you excluded failure from your language?

Father, we cry out for help to love our kids unconditionally like You do, even when they fall and especially when they fall hard. Help us model Your unfailing, merciful grace, so they see Jesus in us and not just hear about Him from us. Praise You, Lord.

THIRTEEN

Faith

If we are faithless, He will remain faithful,
for He cannot disown himself.

—2 TIMOTHY 2:13

What do you do when your child is 1500 miles away at school, down the hall, or in their first apartment, and you sense something is not right? How do you remain peaceful knowing God has got this? Having experienced this uneasiness with both of my young adults, I must admit, I did not like the feelings it evoked in me.

When I experienced these moments and finally saw my child's face and heard his/her voice via *Facetime*, it brought a sense of relief. Technology has its downside; but when it comes to connecting with loved ones who live far away, I am very grateful.

Our faith is continually growing and stretching; and when our children leave home, it might be the most challenging faith cultivator. We will wonder where they are, who they are with, why they haven't called or texted, or if they are being responsible at school or at work. All of these thoughts run through our heads which makes it difficult to trust in God. These concerns will require us to step up our trust, our faith, and our prayers in a way we might not have experienced before. We want certainty, certainty that our children are okay.

For me, knowing that our relationship, their struggle, their successes, their openness, their needs, and who they were becoming was in process, were gifts to me. Did I believe things would be perfect this side of heaven? No, but I knew it would be one day.

I have discovered that when my child is faithless (or I am), God will remain faithful. He will bring about the plans He has for them or me. He will make His purpose known. God has spoken these words of faithfulness to me often. I cling to them and return to them regularly. His promises have brought me great comfort in knowing He has got my children's back. He is leading and guiding them in the way they should go. He is counseling them and watching over them. It is up to my kids to listen to His guidance, His counsel, and to follow His ways. He has given them that choice.

I heard something regarding our children that hit me in a new way. "It is not the taking care of them that is hard, it is the letting go." I agree one hundred percent! Just like our children grow up and move onto the next stage of their lives, we also grow up as they become independent and leave our homes. If you are in that season, how is it going for you?

> It is wise to lovingly accept and encourage our children on their journeys with God. It might not look like you want, but do your best to accept where they are today.

It is not easy being a parent of a teenager/young adult today. They are facing many things we never faced when we were their age. But God is still on the throne, and He is faithful and true. What an opportunity we have to grow and trust God is growing our child's faith. It is wise to lovingly accept and encourage our children on their journeys with God. It might not look like you want, but do your best to accept where they are today.

Understanding your child's personal spiritual values will help you know how to approach or not approach them when it comes to conversations around their faith. It might become sensitive as they figure out what God and faith mean to them. Let them ask questions, and make sure your responses are calm. Then, go and pray that God will meet them exactly where they are today. He will. He is kind, patient, and loving. He has good plans for you and them. Look for ways to practice gratitude; no matter what season your child may be in on their spiritual journey. God does not waste anything.

Be open. Be loving. Be gentle. Be patient. And again, do your best to develop a close and intimate relationship with your teenager/ young adult, sustained by understanding and words that will bear fruit in the years to come. Have faith, faith that He who began the good work in them will bring it to completion. Amen.

Smart Reflection

In what ways is your faith growing? Are you having trouble trusting God with where your child is in his faith? What kinds of talks are you having about their current journey in life? If any? Is it a season to be quiet and pray for opportunities to present themselves?

_____

_____

_____

_____

_____

_____

_____

_____

A New Possibility

What if you stepped back and chose to trust God daily in a way you have not trusted Him before? How would that feel? What if you got quiet on spiritual matters with your kids and placed them at the Father's feet? Will you let Him have His way with them?

Father God, I confess my faith is weak at times. I worry and get anxious about many things concerning my children. I once again surrender them to Your loving protection and care. I believe You've got them. You have told me You've got them. I choose to believe it. I thank You that even when I am faithless, and so are they, You will remain faithful to us. Thank You, Jesus.

FOURTEEN

Freedom

It is for freedom Christ has set us free. Stand firm, then, and do not let
yourselves be burdened again by a yoke of slavery.

—GALATIANS 5:1

How have you been modeling freedom in Christ to your teenager/young adult? Is it possible you could be modeling "religious" behavior?

When our children were growing up, they were expected to attend church, clean their room, be respectful, take care of their responsibilities, like homework, chores, and a countless number of other things. Sometimes they got it right, and sometimes they did not.

When they left our home, it then became their choice to decide about the many options thrown at them. The struggle within my own heart emerged when they did things differently than they had been taught. I (we) could no longer control or require them to submit to our way of thinking and doing. When I (we) did, it didn't go well.

You may say, "But Patti, you still hold the purse strings." And you would be correct. You could also assume my children are not financially independent. All true. However, the bottom line is this: they are going to do what they want, when they want, and how they

> When teens/young adults are given freedom to choose, there are bound to be differences. They are figuring out life, and it will take patience, grace, and love on our part to let them.

want. It is our human nature and flesh that fights to do its own thing. We do not like to be told what to do. When teens/young adults are given freedom to choose, there are bound to be differences. They are figuring out life, and it will take patience, grace, and love on our part to let them.

Their desire for growing independence and freedom are God-given. As a parent of a young adult, do they have certain requirements? What are the *must do's*? What choices do they have now that they are out on their own (but most likely still financially dependent on you)?

As Christians, our hearts' desire is for our children to experience the life and love of Jesus without interruption as they grow into young adults. Despite our hopes, when it comes to spiritual matters, they may go out and test the waters, take a break from church, or question how they have been raised. Consider this: there is no formula to shore up their relationship with Jesus without adding complications. The last thing you want is to sever communication with your child, especially if they are living away from home. The fact of the matter is this: it is God who does the sustaining, not us. He runs after our hearts to rescue us from us. Having said that, there are practical ways to help facilitate or mentor young people in their growth as believers. Ask God how you can best reach their heart. How that unfolds will look different for each of your children.

My husband, Frank, has modeled freedom to my children and me in the most admirable way. He clearly understands that the love, grace, and the favor of God extends to us because of what Jesus did for us, not what we did/do for Him. It is difficult to model freedom to our teenagers/young adults, but it is possible.

Until people grasp the law of God, it is challenging for them to understand the grace and freedom that comes through an intimate and personal relationship with Jesus. When we realize that the law of God is not within reach, it exposes our hearts. We cannot keep the law. This is why Jesus came. There is nothing left for us to do except believe in the one God sent—Jesus.

One of the ways I modeled freedom in my relationship with Jesus was to tell my kids of my brokenness and great need for Him. I have yelled at my children, been angry, said things I have regretted, and so on. However, God gave me grace to repent and ask for forgiveness each and every time. I remember specifically telling both Ryan and Hope, "Do you see how much I need Jesus too?" I daily need His grace.

All of us need to become cognizant of God's standard. Once we do this and recognize we cannot live up to it, grace can enter in.

Freedom in our home looks like this—watching church online, missing quiet times, missing prayer at mealtime, on occasion speaking not-so-nice words and then asking for forgiveness, choosing to spend time with a hurting friend instead of going to Bible study, spending endless hours reading God's Word, praying, reading a Christian book instead of my Bible, listening to worship music instead of sitting quietly in the morning, or driving to a meeting and praying on the way.

There is no method to a *free* life in Christ. It is Spirit led. There may be times freedom may mean listening quietly to a friend who has a different set of beliefs than yours. Listen is the key word. If your friend is not born-again spiritually, build a relationship for an opportunity to share the good news of Jesus. Let them know that forgiveness, deliverance, and peace are only found in Him.

Take some time to reflect over the next few days. Actions speak louder than your words. Teenagers and young adults see clearly when your beliefs don't align with what you preach. They will be quick to call you out on your misdeeds. I've been there. Do yourself a favor and ask God to reveal any blind spots in your life. Modeling freedom with intentionality will be a game-changer and produce a great dividend for all of your lives.

💬 SMART REFLECTION

What does it mean to you to be under the grace of God and not the law of God? In what ways are you building a religious life as opposed to building a relationship with Jesus?

_____

_____

_____

_____

_____

_____

_____

_____

A NEW POSSIBILITY

What if you set your young adults free—free to discover for themselves the life, love, and grace of Jesus? What if you were on board with them exploring their faith and looking for answers for themselves, not just settling for a secondhand version of something handed down to them? And what if they gave you the privilege of processing those thoughts with them? What if you didn't tell and sell your faith, but listened in new way to connect to your children and their growth process?

Lord, help me to live out the grace of God in front of my teenagers/young adults. Prompt me on how to best model the grace given to me time and time again. Thank You, Jesus.

FIFTEEN

Gaps

I will teach all your children. And they will enjoy great peace.

—Isaiah 54:13

D o you ever feel as though you might have missed teaching your teenager/young adult something important before they head out into the world? Are there any life lessons, extra-curricular activities, leadership, or serving opportunities that you regret not giving them? If you are like me, your answer most likely is yes. Here is what I'd love to tell you—it is going to be okay. The God of the universe will step in and fill in the places you missed that are crucial for their lives. He will provide friends, teachers, mentors, and bosses to give your children exactly what they need for this journey called Life. So, take a deep breath. Let it go. And commit your child into the hands of the One who can take them from point A to point Z. He is able to arrange every single essential resource for this life and the next.

I homeschooled my children through the seventh grade with much assistance from others. I had the privilege of being part of a homeschool moms' group, where we had a mentor named Teena. Teena is an insightful, life-giving woman who encouraged and coached us about many topics. One day she posed the same question I asked above, "Do you feel you might miss teaching your child certain important lessons or skills for life or fail to provide them an opportunity for growth?" The moms present in the room that night resounded loudly, "YES!" As homeschool moms, we were anxious that we might omit important learnings regarding our children's studies. Home education is a huge responsibility and undertaking. But when you know God has called you to instruct your children at home, and He confirms it, it is wise to obey Him.

What Teena told us that evening brought me and others the much needed freedom and peace for the years ahead. She continued, "You will miss things. However, God is faithful to fill in the gaps."

> "You will miss things. However, God is faithful to fill in the gaps."

When we have a mindset that provides everything under the sun for our children, we leave no room for God to equip them with what they truly need. We tend to put a lot of pressure on ourselves to supply their wishes and wants, instead of nudging them toward God. Transitioning dependence on you to dependence on God is a must. Beginning this process in the teen years will transfer the burden of responsibility to their relationship with God and you as a soundboard. Allowing our kids to grapple with the gap areas in their life and then go to God for answers will build character and provide valuable lessons for the coming days. When we do this and do it well, we give God the opportunity to make Himself known. Do they need a part-time job, better ACT or SAT scores, the latest fashions, a new computer, or the latest iPhone? Do they really need these things, or are they comparing and despairing because of what everyone else is doing, wearing, or owning?

We want them to have needs. This is worth repeating. We want them to have needs. When they have needs, they get to feel lack, they experience something missing. If you rush in to provide for those needs, you will deprive your child of earning a buck, studying harder, helping a friend, and so on. By not having everything they want, they may realize they can live without the latest and the greatest. And most importantly, a need allows them the chance to ask God to provide for them. Without needs, they will not need God. Let them hunger.

As moms, we have many needs, which in turn, causes us to be dependent on God. It is the same with our teenager/young adults. If we don't let them experience need, we are setting them up for hurdles in the future. Be purposeful about what you teach your teenager/young adult, but allow room for growth. Our children develop into responsible, hard-working, and contributing citizens in our world by discerning real needs from frivolous wants.

Both my children struggled with figuring out budgets, schooling, dating, careers, being on their own, and taking care of daily responsibilities. I was there to encourage them, but not to do it for them. The wrestling with the gaps in their life produces strength of character. God has shown up with financial planners to assist with budgeting, friends and roommates to teach more about cooking, other moms to talk about dating, bosses to show them about great systems and habits in the workplace, and so on.

God is faithful when we have either dropped the ball or have not had the skill to teach our children. We can always count on God to fill in the gaps—again and again.

Pray and ask God if you might be interfering too much with their needs. Each child's needs are different, and you may or may not be the best person to meet them. Be confident God will provide for your children in ways He sees fit. What might be good for one child is not for the other. Accept this. It will give you peace and a calm in knowing your Heavenly Father has good plans and purposes for their future.

Smart Reflection

What gaps did you miss? What are you aware of that God needs to fill in for your child? Will you ask God to make it clear so you can pray for provision?

_____

_____

_____

_____

_____

_____

_____

_____

_____

 ## A New Possibility

What if God made Himself known by filling in some huge gap in your child's life? What if a friend or mentor was placed on her path to teach her study skills, cooking skills, budgeting, or whatever else she is lacking but needs in her current season of life?

Father I thank You that You are the great Provider! Please help me to be at peace with the existing gaps that I see present today. Help me to trust You in a new way and believe that You have got my child, and You will be there to meet her in every way.

SIXTEEN

Hard

Count it all joy, my brothers, when you meet trials of various kinds, for you know that the testing of your faith produces steadfastness. And let steadfastness have its full effect, that you may be perfect and complete, lacking nothing.

—JAMES 1:2-4

Hard means difficult, troublesome, involving a great deal of effort, fatiguing, performing, or carrying on work with great effort. Hard is good. Hard invites us to dig deep. Hard is what builds character, strength, stick-to-it-ness, long-suffering, work ethic, unconditional love, and so many other great character qualities.

With this understanding, do you allow your teenagers and young adults to be hard-pressed with difficult assignments or projects? Or do you run to rescue them? Is your instinct to jump in and fix everything? How do we know when it is appropriate to step in to lend a hand or step back to let them struggle with difficult circumstances, situations, or people in their lives?

I've done both. I've rescued when I should've allowed my children to contend with the issue, and I've let go when I should've stepped in. Either way, we need to ask the Lord what is best for our child in every situation. *Should I assist or should I step back? Will my actions help, hinder, or harm their growth in the situation?* These questions are best left answered by the Lord, when we can take a minute to reflect, breathe, pray, and ask God what is best at this moment—best for all involved—not just for me.

One of the hardest seasons for parents is sending our teenagers off to college or to live out their next chapter. It's hard for us to say goodbye and let go, and hard for them to figure out how to live life without Mom and Dad watching over them.

At 18 years old, my courageous daughter moved to New York City raring to go. She packed her two suitcases (more like five), and off she went to pursue her passion. New York is a long way from our home. Was it hard on all of us? Absolutely. Were my husband and I in agreement that this is where she needed and desired to be? Absolutely. The Lord blew open the doors for her to attend the acting conservatory of her dreams and provided an amazing place to live. All the pieces came together for her quickly. We knew it would be hard to let her leave, but we also knew it was right.

On one of our calls, I asked her how hard it has been. Her response? "Harder than I ever imagined, Mom."

I said, "So how do you do it? How do you stay?"

She said, "I stay because I love it. There is something inside of me that says acting is part of who I am. This is what keeps me here."

Hope is coming home in a few weeks, and I look forward to hearing all about the "hard" she's faced and still faces. I also can't wait to hear how she's overcome.

For me, my daughter's departure for a whole new world created a different kind of hard. It was hard to be away from my baby girl. Hard to connect by phone or *Facetime* on occasion. Hard to control myself, when I wanted to ask fishing questions like, "Where were you last night?" (I can see on her location tracker exactly where she is, but I don't necessarily know what she is doing.) It was hard for me to let go of control and let God write the story of Hope's life.

When my daughter moved out on her own, I wanted so badly to impose my thoughts, beliefs, and ideas about what I thought she should be doing, what friends she should be hanging out with, or why she wasn't in church on Sunday. But I had already done all that for eighteen years. I had done my job. It was now her journey to figure it all out. I had to let go of so much, and by His grace, God taught me how.

He gently spoke to me through his Word, through friends, through songs, and yes, through my own heart. Though the experience has been hard, I can honestly say, I am trusting Him more this year than last, because I believe God's power is greater than any fear or trouble I may face. He can do all things to love, protect, guide, speak, and bring encouragement to both of my children at any time and any place, just as He has done for me. God has given me such peace, and I am grateful.

Hard is good. Hard is necessary. And hard is what hopefully makes us and our kids bend our knee to Jesus and ask for help. When we don't have hard, we don't seek Jesus. Let's choose to get out of His way and let Him do what only He can do in our children's lives, as He does in ours.

Hard is good. Hard is necessary. And hard is what hopefully makes us and our kids bend our knees to Jesus and ask for help.

SMART REFLECTION

How difficult is it to tackle "hard" in your life? What fruit have you seen from pressing into the hard? How about your kids? How do they handle hard? Do you let them?

_____

_____

_____

_____

_____

_____

_____

_____

_____

 ## A NEW POSSIBILITY

What if the next time "hard" found its way into your kids' lives, you gave them a bit of guidance; but you let them evaluate what's best? What if you took your hands off the situation and let them deal with it? How would that feel to you? What could it do for them?

Father, it is difficult at times to let my teenagers fight their own battles or figure out their relationship challenges. So many times, I want to step in. Please give me wisdom to know how to handle the next situation that arises, so my children can be empowered to solve their own problems.

SEVENTEEN

Horizontal—Vertical

Set your minds on things above, not on earthly things.

—COLOSSIANS 3:2

Horizontal: *relating to, directed toward, or consisting of individuals or entities of similar status or on the same level.*

Vertical: *being in a position or direction perpendicular to the plane of the horizon; upright, plumb.*[2]

We all have multiple relationships in our lives, and we engage with a handful daily. What do yours look like?

- Are these relationships generally at peace, or is there too many moments of conflict?

- Have you had an ongoing struggle in marriage?

- Do you and your teenager/young adult have issues you can't seem to resolve?

A verse that comes to mind is James 1:19-20, which says, "My dear brothers and sisters, take note of this. Everyone should be quick to listen, slow to speak and slow to become angry, because human anger does not produce (or bear Holy Spirit fruit) the righteousness that God desires" (NIV).

---

2 https://www.merriam-webster.com

In Chapter 4, James asks, "What is the cause of your conflicts and quarrels with each other? Doesn't the battle begin inside of you as you fight to have your own way and fulfill your own desires?" (James 4:1 TPT).

These verses are convicting, and yet they encourage us to recognize what is happening in our own hearts. Take time to think about those relationships that you can't seem to make right. Looking inward first could help solve the conflict.

I realize relationships are messy and not easy at times; however, God has given us a book of instruction to guide us as we relate to one another. My experience has been this: when my relationship with God (vertical) is fresh, moving, and growing, my horizontal relationships tend to move, grow, and improve. The opposite is also true. When things are not going well horizontally, you might want to check your vertical relationship.

Sometimes, maybe all the time, and maybe never, it is difficult to connect with your spouse or young adult. They are too busy, you are too busy, or they won't put their phones down. Do your conversations with your teenager last more than one minute? Then you know what I am talking about. I had one teen that told me everything, and one that pretty much told me nothing.

As I sought the Lord for wisdom, love, and guidance (vertical inquiries), He provided answers (horizontal prompts). We raised our teenagers in the best way we knew how. We taught them to walk in honesty, integrity, responsibility, and a deep love for God. We knew God's ways worked, and we expected our children to follow. Each child was different, and what God asked me to do or say with one child was not the same as what He had me say or do for the other. The beauty was that it kept me on my knees and praying continually—often in my master bedroom closet.

God understands my children better than I do. But when I was raising them, I had to choose daily to get myself in the presence of Jesus, so He could share instruction and insight. Knowing how to be in relationship (mood swings and all) with my teenager/young adult was like putting

> Knowing how to be in relationship (mood swings and all) with my teenager/young adult was like putting together a puzzle with no picture on the box.

together a puzzle with no picture on the box. Sometimes I did this well, and sometimes I did not. Thank goodness for the mercy of God and both of my children, who have always shown me grace when it comes to my mess ups.

Today, I still rely on the Holy Spirit to teach me the optimal time for approaching a subject or sitting down and talking through a particular situation. As I depend on the Holy Spirit (my vertical relationship), He helps me navigate the horizontal relationships in my life.

I honestly don't know how parents find solutions for issues they face with their teenager/young adult without God. Finding a safe community of faith support is critical to our sanity, as we love our young adults through the transition of this growth season. My husband and I are part of a small group at our church, and the camaraderie, perspective, and comfort we receive are invaluable parts of our lives. We were created for horizontal relationships with faith-filled people, but you must first start vertically. If you don't have a relationship with God, you can very simply invite Him into your life by praying this prayer.

> *Lord Jesus, I need You. Please forgive me for my failures, mistakes and sins. I invite You into my life and heart to make me the kind of person you desire*

me to be. I believe Jesus is who He says He is. I also
believe the only unforgiveable sin is rejection of Jesus.
Lord, I accept You and receive You into my life right
now. Amen.

Now go tell someone you took a huge and important first step to connect vertically, so you can have more help and peace horizontally in life, love, and all of your relationships.

Smart Reflection

What surfaced inside of you after reading this devotion? What is one step you could take today to make things right with God and others?

_____

_____

_____

_____

_____

_____

_____

_____

 ## A New Possibility

What if you planned out your time with God every day and made Him a priority? How would that change your relationships for the better? Would it?

Thank You, Jesus, that it is never too late to begin again. Thank You that you give second, third, and fourth chances in life. I am grateful for Your never-ending love and presence. Help me to spend time with You listening and getting to know You more intimately each and every day through Your Word. My desire is to be on good terms with the people I love and care about the most.

EIGHTEEN

Identity

I have been crucified with Christ and I no longer live,
but Christ lives in me.

—GALATIANS 2:20

In parenting my young adult children, I found this season to be one of the most challenging times, especially for them. Having raised one teenage boy and finishing up raising my teenage girl, I saw identity take center stage between the ages of thirteen and nineteen, and a little beyond.

Every teen on the planet asks themselves: *Who am I in this phase of life? Will I be liked? How do I look? Should I wear makeup? Will I make the team? Am I good enough? Why don't I have any good friends? Should I hang out with these friends who are making poor choices? Can I look at these illicit pictures just once? What will they think of me?* My heart's desire for them is to not only ask "Who am I?" but "Who do I want to be?"

Your teenagers can easily fall into the trap of pleasing, appeasing to be accepted, or both. They can choose to be someone other than who God created them to be when under pressure to conform to cultural norms. We should remind our teenager/young adult that Romans 12:2 encourages us to renew our minds with thoughts and ideas that would bring honor to God. When we do this, and they do this, we will know God's will and who we are in Him. This is a foundational truth our kids can take with them into their day and throughout their life.

Who are you? and *Who do you want to be?* are great questions to leave your children with as they jump out of the car or walk out the door. When you send them out into the world, hopefully they will remember these two simple questions. Beginning this practice early by communicating it verbally, leaving a note in their lunch, leaving a scripture verse by their pillow, or sending them a song that conveys this truth, will reinforce God's Word and plant it deep in their soul.

The Bible says in Isaiah 55:11, "So is My word that goes out from My mouth: it will not return to Me empty" (NIV). I stand on that truth. When my children were in their tweens (ages nine to twelve), my husband and I kept a journal with each of them. We took turns writing back and forth with our children, penning encouragement, fun memories, and the truth of God's Word. It was fun when the journal arrived on our pillow or in another spot of the house where we spent time. This was a special way to pour into our kids and remind them of our unconditional love and acceptance.

During times of struggle and uncertainty, battles with our teenagers seem more common than ever. They face so much. Being present to help them process through all the muck of the world will be a gift to them. As they continue to figure out their identity (hopefully in Christ), and who God is, your presence and attention is of the utmost priority.

My prayer is that you have separated who they are from their behavior, especially as teenagers. Speaking into their lives during this critical time is central. The opinions of their peers and acceptance by their friends usually takes precedence over Mom and Dad. Calling out their greatness (their unique self, gifts, talents, and skills) and asking questions to help them discover their identity in Christ will make for great conversation, bond you, and impact your kids for years to come.

> Calling out their greatness (their unique self, gifts, talents, and skills) and asking questions to help them discover their identity in Christ will make for great conversation, bond you, and impact your kids for years to come.

A friend of mine shared a story with me about her teenage son who was treating her with disrespect. She called me from her own self-imposed "time-out" to give me the details and ask for prayer. She locked herself in a closet to hide from her son. We talked and prayed it through. She later went back to him to let him know calmly that she would not allow him to speak to her rudely or disrespectfully. She told him this was not who God created him to be. She said in God's eyes he was a respectful young man, but he was not behaving as such. She wanted to encourage him to live in a way that honored and respected God, herself, and others in his life.

At that point, her son broke down and cried. He let her know he had a rough day at school, and he was struggling on the inside with a myriad of feelings. They ended up having an open, honest, and sensitive conversation that led to reconciliation and a stronger connection in their relationship. My friend was able to separate the behavior from who her son was, and as a result it created a space for him to open up and become vulnerable.

In my own parenting, I've had to step back and choose not to react to comments or behavior and ask the Holy Spirit for wisdom. He delivers each time, and His answer is usually "be quiet." Keeping my comments and opinions to myself has saved me many times from more drama and conflict. I wish I had learned this earlier in my parenting, rather than later.

For the teenager, it is all about the "haves" and the "have nots." It's mostly about the outer appearance—clothes, phones, social media, cars, computers, the right shoes, nails, hair, watches, and more. Some of us never grow out of that pressure. If you are trapped by *things*, please find a way out. As adults, we know material possessions do not satisfy us. The appearance of having it all together, and all that comes with it, is exhausting. Having a beautiful appearance, along with a right and God-revering heart, is empowering.

When you become the person who God created you to be and understand your identity, you will progressively do and be who God says you are, more consistently over time. Identity determines purpose. Purpose determines mission. Mission brings fulfillment.

Know who you are, and remind your teenager and young adult who they are "in Christ." When they deviate, you can say to them, "Johnny, that is not who God called you to be. You are a strong, courageous, and faith-filled man. Now go and be that every single day." Show them you are their biggest fan. Plant seeds of life, love, and hope, and watch those seeds sprout in God's time and according to His agenda, not yours.

SMART REFLECTION

What would you like to discuss with God about your identity in Him? How have you settled the identity issue in your own life? Would you settle it today?

_____

_____

_____

_____

_____

_____

_____

_____

 ## A NEW POSSIBILITY

What if you accepted wholeheartedly who you are in Christ, and you were able to model that in the most beautiful way to your teenager and young adult? How would that change things for you and for them?

Lord, let me continually seek You and sit with You, so I may know beyond a shadow of a doubt who I am, who You are, and live my life accordingly. Thank You, Lord, for showing me with great clarity that what is on the inside is always expressed clearly on the outside. Praise You.

NINETEEN

Jobs

Whatever you do, work heartily, as for the Lord and not for men.

—Colossians 3:23

What kind of value do you place on your teenager/young adult about working in high school or when they go off to college? What kind of work ethic did your family of origin exhibit? Is work experience necessary or important for your teenager/young adult before they leave your home?

My husband and I discussed the work topic prior to our children entering high school. Being like-minded on this subject is important. You might say, "My teenager has no time for work. They attend school all day, participate in a team sport, take dance class after school, and then work on a ton of homework. I barely see them now."

Your spouse might think differently about the idea of work for your teenager. They might think it is better for him/her to develop a work ethic from a job and a boss, as opposed to extra-curricular activity. Either way, look for ways in which you can build excellent work ethics into your child's character—either on the job, at home, or both.

As you think through your own beliefs and values about work, what would you like to teach your teenager/young adult regarding a job well done? What character qualities are important for them to take into the workplace one day?

My son started his first job at sixteen. It was a hard job with physical labor. When he arrived home from school each day, he would head to the tire shop to work a few hours. They paid him well; however, he ran into some challenges along the way, giving us the opportunity to instruct him through the issue. Without a job, we would not have been able to coach and mentor him through some painful situations that arose while working there. He ended up walking away with integrity and grace, which he has taken with him into all of his other places of employment.

If it works for your family, do your teen a favor, and give him/her the opportunity of having a boss, being accountable to someone other than you or your spouse, and serving other people. Let them experience putting the phone away and focusing on something else besides video games, *YouTube*, *Instagram*, *Snapchat*, *Facebook*, *TikTok*, or the latest *Netflix* series.

Both of our children worked before they left the nest, and they came home with all kinds of stories about the people they worked with, or the customers they encountered. This made for great conversations, learning experiences, and teachable moments. Character building was among the lessons learned in shaping their work ethic. It was challenging for them at times, yes; but we would not have had it any other way. My daughter was given the option to graduate high school early through an online program, and she was able to save a substantial amount of money for her move to New York City that coming September.

I came from a family of blue-collar workers with a great work ethic. Both my mom and dad were exemplary employees who brought value to their employers. My dad was a bricklayer, and my mom was a crossing guard, who eventually worked in security.

Watching my single mom work two jobs was an important lesson for me. There were no handouts for my mom, Barbara, just hard work to make ends meet. And she never complained, was never sick, or ever missed work. She was up early and off to her job, so she could take care of my sister and me. We were both teenagers at the time, and we needed to work ourselves to pay for some of the things she could not afford. There wasn't a lot left over from Mom's paycheck, so my sister and I usually bought most of our own clothes. I went without some of my wants, but not the most important things.

I'm glad for the insights about work ethics I discovered as a teenager. Those lessons have carried me through my adulthood and helped me succeed in ways I had not imagined. Figuring out the best processes for your child to gain the skills necessary for great work ethics is something you can determine one child at a time.

For our children, encouraging and requiring them to work provided them with experiences outside our home. They gained skills, friendships, knowledge, and discipline—all of which they still use. Today, they have grown into responsible and hard-working adults.

Contributing to something bigger than ourselves, whether it be work or ministry, helps define who we are and what we are made of. We figure out what we like and what we don't. Introducing our children to different professions or ministries could prove valuable for discovery of a career or mission they never thought about. Take some time to think through your values and beliefs regarding your child working before they enter high school. You'll be glad you did.

> Contributing to something bigger than ourselves, whether it be work or ministry, helps define who we are and what we are made of.

SMART REFLECTION

What is the best way to initiate a discussion with your spouse about your values based on your work ethics?

_____

_____

_____

_____

_____

_____

_____

_____

_____

 ## A NEW POSSIBILITY

What if your teenagers/young adults tried their hand at something entrepreneurial, where they could work around the family and school schedule? Would you consider exploring this idea with them? What could they gain from such an experience?

Lord, lead us and guide us in the way we should go in regard to whether or not it would be beneficial to our teenagers/young adults to hold a job before they leave our home. Thank You that You always make a way and shape them into the people they are becoming.

TWENTY

Leadership

Don't let anyone look down on you because you are young,
but set an example for the believers in speech, in conduct,
in love, in faith and in purity.

—1 TIMOTHY 4:12

I first heard the words "you don't have to wait to be great" at my home church. It immediately resonated with me, because I am passionate about equipping and mentoring others to reach the best version of themselves. God has placed unique gifts and talents inside each of us, and it is our mission, with the help of the Holy Spirit, to live up to the potential woven inside each of us.

Speaking into young people's lives is paramount at our church. This concept is so important, they have dedicated an entire *next gen* weekend for the purposes of creating the leaders of tomorrow. Once a year they give high schoolers the opportunity to serve the church in various capacities at our weekend services. These young adults greet, lead worship, help with production, serve coffee, and usher people to their seats.

Giving teens and young adults the honor to serve is not an after-thought but an intentional forethought to help develop them into the influencers of tomorrow. Their involvement in making a difference is both impactful and life-changing for the teen and for those on the receiving end. 'You don't have to wait to be great" is a brilliant idea and worth duplicating in other churches, ministries, businesses, and at home. So, let me ask you, in what ways are you guiding the development of the leader in your teenager/young adult? What kinds of teachable moments are you introducing them to, so they may gain mastery skills?

> Giving teens and young adults the honor to serve is not an afterthought but an intentional forethought to help develop them into the influencers of tomorrow.

Both of my children participated in programs through their high school, where they were required to write papers on leadership and serve in local ministries. At the culmination of the year, they attended a memorable trip, where they were given the privilege of touring historical sites, as well as attending workshops and training on becoming a servant leader. In addition to school, they had opportunities to lead at church through our Disciple Now program and in weekly services. Instilling a service mindset and providing giving-back moments has made a difference, as they stepped up through volunteering.

Servant leadership has the ability to make a significant difference on young lives. It blesses those being cared for, and enables those serving to possibly discover a natural bent they had not known prior to the experience. In the words of Jesus, "It is more blessed to give than receive," a true statement that will bring joy and happiness to our lives.

John Maxwell says, "Leadership is influence." This quote causes me to reflect upon ways we can teach our children to influence others as teenagers and young adults. To begin with, character is foundational. Merriam-Webster defines character as "the mental and moral qualities distinctive to an individual."

A few years back, a life coach asked me a question: "How well do you lead yourself?"

It was a simple prompt that caused a profound impact on my heart and life. Nobody is going to call me up in the morning and tell me what to do with my day. As a leader, I must decide the important and not-so-important choices to be made for the moment. Taking time to reflect on this concept can change what your life looks like today and in the years to come. What feelings or thoughts come to mind when you think about leading yourself? Are you willing to be led? Have your children seen the self-discipline you have developed in leading yourself in certain areas of your life?

Leading ourselves is no doubt a challenge. Without dependence on the Holy Spirit and His guidance, it is impossible. We must be *willing* to first choose for ourselves a place where trust, authenticity, and vulnerability are evident character qualities and part of the fabric of our lives, before we are ever able to lead, influence, and have a lasting impression on our teenager or young adult.

Who is that one person in your life you can ask, "Do you think I lead myself well? And how do you feel I respond to being led?" A good place to begin is with the people with whom we feel safe and trust. Their response will give you a good indication on how to adjust your journey as an influencer of your teens/young adults. Reading books on leadership, listening to podcasts, joining a book study club, or hiring a coach will help you move toward the next level, as you learn to apply the concepts of leadership.

I will leave you with this profound thought by Thomas à Kempis: "Be not angry that you cannot make others as you wish them to be, since you cannot make yourself as you wish to be." Learning to lead ourselves first will provide evidence others want to follow from the *fruit* in our lives. As our young adults watch us, more will be caught than taught—every single time.

💬 SMART REFLECTION

Take some time to revisit the question, "How well do I lead myself?" How can you better equip your teens and young adults to become self-governing as they move into adulthood? Will you ask God?

_____

_____

_____

_____

_____

_____

_____

_____

 ## A NEW POSSIBILITY

What if you paid attention to how you are leading yourself daily? What if your young adults saw the difference and asked about it? What would you say? What practical examples could you give them to show them how this has made a difference in your life?

Thank You, Lord, that You have given us the Holy Spirit as our Helper. Search me, Oh God, and show me how I can lead myself well. I pray my teens would see it and ask about it. I pray I could be open, honest, and authentic about my own struggles and challenges with this concept.

TWENTY-ONE

Letting Go

Forget the former things; do not dwell on the past.
See, I am doing a new thing!

—Isaiah 43:18-19

What does it look like for you to let go of your teenager/young adult and let God take the reins of their life? Has it been difficult? Maybe you haven't sent your son or daughter off to college or their new adventure, but you are preparing for this season.

I became a "helicopter" college mom when my eighteen-year-old daughter moved to New York City. I hovered. Allowing our daughter to move to one of the biggest cities in the world was a bit overwhelming at times. It was not easy to surrender my child into God's care. Though familiar with the phrase "Let go and let God," at first, I was successful at neither one.

My daughter took on the city like the champion she is. She was fearless from the start—riding the subways, figuring out rideshares, heading into the outer boroughs with her friends, food shopping (which in NYC, is no easy task), and did all the things adulting requires. Figuring out laundry, memorizing tons of lines for her scenes at school, and being one of the youngest students at the conservatory had its ups and downs. I asked her how she was. "Mom,

I'm thriving," she said. "I miss you and Dad, but I am good. I love New York City!"

I was happy she was adjusting well and doing so quickly, but I did not share her happiness. Don't get me wrong, I wasn't crying myself to sleep at night or pouting on the couch all day; it was just a big adjustment on many levels.

My daughter and I have a candid, honest, and growing relationship, and I couldn't be more grateful. But this came as a result of a choice. We continually love through the tears, forgive and forget, start over each day, and refuse to allow the enemy a foothold in our lives.

When your child has her/his location services turned on, the temptation to check their location whenever they are not in school can feel overwhelming. When I did this, it only produced anxiety and worried thoughts. *Why are you in Brooklyn? Why are you in upstate New York, and who are you with? What time did you get home? I saw you were out late. Whose house were you at?*

Sometimes, I randomly asked the next day, "How was your night?"

I was fishing when I really wanted to say, "Tell me the truth, what did you really do last night? Were you at a party? Who was there, and were you partying too?"

> In demanding control, we remove God from the equation.

I hated all the emotions my insecurity evoked in me. I made a lot of assumptions and judgments that drove me nuts. When I finally spoke with my daughter, it didn't always go well. I had already decided what she had been doing or not been doing that weekend, though most of the time none of it was true. I encourage you not to make those same mistakes. Smothering is not a choice that will produce life and love in the relationship with your child. In demanding control, we remove God from the equation. We must decide to believe He has our children in His care, or He does not. Choose trust.

Eventually, I got the hang of distance-parenting through lots of discussion and tears with both God and my daughter. We figured out the new normal and adjusted. Was it easy? No. But because my heart's desire was to stay in an honest and candid conversation with her, I made the all-important shift. I also repented.

Parenting is work. It's hard. Thankfully, God was ever so faithful to speak to me and encourage me in my new season as an empty nester. He is so good to meet us and love us where we are, not where we think we should be. As we reach out to Him, He shows up again and again, and He graciously guides us along the way.

As you go about your day and pray for your children, present your petitions to God and thank Him. Thank Him that He has got you. Thank Him that He's got them. Thank Him that He is turning up in their lives in ways where they would recognize His care.

SMART REFLECTION

How are you struggling to let go of control and trust God with your child? What scripture verse do you need to write on a Post-It® note as a reminder of His love and care for your child? When I left my daughter in Harlem for her second year at school, the Lord led me to this verse: "The LORD will watch over her coming and going both now and forevermore" (Ps. 121:8 (NIV).

_____

_____

_____

_____

_____

_____

_____

 ## A NEW POSSIBILITY

What if you spoke words of life over your child that said: "I trust you. You've got this. You will make the right decision. I am here for you. Keep trusting Jesus through it all"? How do you think that might feel for her and you?

Father, it is not easy for me to let go after so many years of hanging on. But today, I choose to trust You and believe that You can take better care of my child than I ever could. My worrying gets me nowhere. Help me to have faith as she ventures out into new places. I pray You would send godly, Jesus-loving people into her life. I am grateful for Your love and protection.

TWENTY-TWO

Master

If you declare with your mouth, "Jesus is Lord," and believe in your heart that God raised Him from the dead, you will be saved.

—ROMANS 10:9-10

Who is your master? What is your mission? Who is your mate? These are the most important questions we can ask ourselves and our children. Internal checks determine who or what governs us, the convictions we live by, who and what we prioritize, what we do, and who we will marry. The first of the three questions is the most important. We will look at *What is your mission?* and *Who is your mate?* in another section; but the answers to these questions and others flow from *Who is your master?*

The word *master* can be defined as one having authority over another—a ruler or governor. This seat of authority in each of us is reserved for the person or thing to which we submit our lives—the person or thing in which we invest our faith, our hardiest trust, and what governs our decisions, great or small. And it's a seat reserved for God alone.

God is master over my life, directing and reigning as I submit to Him on a daily basis (and even if I don't). He rules whether I cooperate or not. My heart's desire is to bend my knee to Him as an act of submission, in every moment, to His lordship in my life.

Teenagers and young adults face many decisions that they need to make socially, culturally, academically, and relationally, to name a few. The answer to *Who is my master?* will determine the choices they make and how they make them, both good and bad. But as a parental authority, you have influence.

Are you encouraging your kids to ask God all kinds of questions? Do you demonstrate belief in Him for answers? Do you remind them to seek God's counsel on questions like these: *Should I attend college or take a year off? What college should I attend? How do I resolve conflicts with others? Should I date this person?*

Your task is to not only ask your children, "Who is your master?" Help them shape the answer. When God reveals the answers to their questions and prayers, it will provide faith-building experiences they won't forget.

One of the best things we can do for our children is to consistently nudge them toward God. Leaning on the Holy Spirit for guidance in every and any situation is smart. He provides guidance for us: the strategies we employ, the words we choose, the pressure we apply, when to prod, when to push, and so on. He will also impart wisdom for our children.

We can only hear the Holy Spirit successfully if God is our master. The exchanges with our kids reflect the exchanges between God and us. We can't be responsible for every choice our child makes, but we can take responsibility for directing them toward the One who has all the answers. We will not always be around. The more we can help our children transition to dependence on God while under our roof, the better their adulthoods will turn out.

> The exchanges with our kids reflect the exchanges between God and us.

When we encourage our kids to rely on the Master, instead of assuming and pushing our need to govern, we empower them for a lifelong and intimate relationship with the Creator of the world. If exchanges with our children mirror governance by the same God, who we hope governs them, it creates a kind of rule of submission. We set an example of revering God, and in turn, we teach our children to respect Him and us.

Explain to your teenager/young adult your own path to surrender, the struggles, and the victories you've had. Reveal the questions you've asked the Lord, and how He answered. Being vulnerable and open can change everything. It is a great model when appropriate, and it often allows you to share your opinions and thoughts in a non-threatening way.

When my kids were young, they always knew where to find me in the morning—in the closet, reading my Bible, praying, and communing with God. I was blessed that they could see my relationship with the Lord in a real and tangible way. I can remember the time my daughter read my journal from when I was her age. She was amazed to realize I had experienced some of the very same things she was going through at the time. This meant a lot to her as a maturing young woman. She felt normal and not crazy for thinking some of the things she was experiencing.

Reflect on a recent conversation you've had with your young adult or teen, and ask yourself if you are aiding in the transition to dependence on God. Better yet, ask the Lord how you are handling their necessary rite of passage. When we submit these kinds of questions to the Master, He is sure to answer in His gracious and truthful way. We can then be confident we are walking in step with His Spirit and helping our children learn to do the same.

💬 SMART REFLECTION

In what ways are you carving out time with your teen to discuss with
him his full dependence on God to lead him in the days to come?
What does that look like, and how is he responding? If he is an older
teen or young adult who has left the house, you may want to add
this to your conversations: "May I share my thoughts?" Be prepared.
Sometimes you get a no, but sometimes it is a yes. If you receive a
no, then leave the circumstance alone and entrust it to God.

_____

_____

_____

_____

_____

_____

_____

A NEW POSSIBILITY

What if you took your hands off your child's decision-making process, knowing you have taught him well and trusting that God can
reveal His plans and answer him clearly?

*Lord, help me to remain keenly aware of how I am helping my teenager/
young adult transition into adulthood. Help me to live open-handed
and give him a voice to ask questions during this passage of time, to
empower him for future decisions. Help me to let go and put those
choices into his hands, so he can learn and grow with You. I pray he
would call on You, God, to make You Lord and Savior of his life.*

TWENTY-THREE

Mission

For this reason, I remind you to fan into flame the gift of God,
which is in you through the laying on of my hands.

—2 TIMOTHY 1:6

As our young adult children were deciding what their next steps were after high school, we asked them, "What is your mission in life? Have you asked God about it?" We encouraged both of our children to not waste time trying to figure it out on their own. We let them know that God clearly has answers for them. Our task was to ask the question, then remain open and listen.

One of the tools we used in helping our children find out their mission was *StrengthsFinder*. *StrengthsFinder* is an assessment tool that helps identify areas of great potential, so we can choose wisely how and where to steward our gifts and talents given to us by God. Both of our children worked through the assessment. The results came back, and they affirmed what we already knew.

Ryan is a strong, determined, influential, and out-going leader designed to create an impact in this world. His friendly disposition makes him loved by many. Hope's strengths lead her to be an empathetic, courageous developer who is a maximizer of all things she loves. Excellence is in her blood. She is an artist who cares about others deeply and supports them unequivocally.

A word of caution here: things like personality tests and such are all great for a snapshot of who we are, but do not widen the lens of the whole picture. We all evolve and change as we grow and mature. With the help of the Holy Spirit, we are all developing into who God desires us to be. When we get stuck and focused on one snapshot, we leave little room for God. Assessments and tests are useful, but they can label and limit people as they pursue their passions and dreams. We don't want to lock our kids into a certain type of personality. Too many individuals get stuck and never move forward into what God wants for them. God's purpose includes moving us beyond what we could ever ask or imagine. If the assessment test is the end-all, we can fixate on what was highlighted and use excuses to stay where we are.

We don't want to hold back our children in any way. I say that to encourage you and open up a space for God to work on what could be. As I've said, never in a million years did I ever think about or even consider writing a book. It was not on my radar, but it certainly was on God's. I barely got out of high school. I only attended college for one year, and I don't consider myself someone who could even write a book. My main aspirations are to love and honor God with my life and help others do the same. However, I do consider myself a smart and high-capacity life-long learner, who is intentional about personal, spiritual, and professional growth. I am continually on a quest to develop myself; so in turn, I can develop others. As I have remained open to His guidance, He has supplied the words and people to come alongside me in this journey. He will do the same for your kids.

Give your teenager/young adult time and margin to grow as a person. When and if they choose Jesus as their master and ask Him about their mission, they have an option to do the impossible, unlimited by what some test or score might have said.

Sometimes those in charge of leading and guiding our children don't always get it right. I remember a friend of mine whose daughter applied for several colleges. The high school guidance counselor told my friend's daughter she would not get into any of the schools she applied for. The daughter was directed to return to the guidance counselor's office when she received her denial letters. The counselor informed her that she could write a letter of recommendation once she had the denial letters in hand. As you can imagine, this was discouraging to both the daughter and the parents. I am happy to say the daughter was accepted to all the colleges she applied to, and she did not need any further recommendations. Let this encourage you.

Stay open. Have faith. Believe God has the very best in mind for your young adult. Help him live up to his God-designed potential: emotionally, spiritually, intellectually, academically, physically, and professionally. Provide opportunities for him to explore his passions, gifts, and desires. The outcome might look different than you expect but go with God. Don't listen to what the world says about your teenager's future—its opinions about his "should" or "shouldn'ts." Don't even go with what you think he should do or be. Follow God. Nurture and affirm your child's heart. Then watch God unfold the beautiful story He has for him.

> Help him live up to his God-designed potential: emotionally, spiritually, intellectually, academically, physically, and professionally.

💬 Smart Reflection

Have you predetermined what your teenager/young adult's mission is in life? Have you given her a safe space to be open and honest about what she really wants to do; both personally and professionally? In her opinion, is she truly free to be honest? Is her mission your dream or hers?

_____

_____

_____

_____

_____

_____

_____

_____

 A New Possibility

What if you had a conversation that went something like this: "Susie, if you had the opportunity and the resources to do anything you wanted after high school, what would it be?" Allowing her to think outside the box without restrictions of resources may give you a glimpse into something you had not known before.

Lord, keep me from imposing what I think my child should do or be in life. Help me listen closely to what she is saying. Help me to be free enough to let go of my dreams for her and embrace Your dreams and desires for her. I trust You will get her to where she needs to be. Amen.

TWENTY-FOUR

Mate

"Do not be yoked together with unbelievers. For what do righteousness and wickedness have in common?

—2 CORINTHIANS 6:14

B oth my children are single and have not yet found their spouses. Though neither Ryan nor Hope know who that right mate is, I have nonetheless prayed and will continue to pray for their life partner until that day arrives. I trust God will make great provision for them and clearly reveal who that individual will be. Marrying the person of God's choosing, and knowing it is God's intent, makes all the difference, especially in the tough times of marriage.

I want to encourage you to design (simple is best) an environment where it's safe to have a multitude of small and big conversations about who your child chooses to marry, as well as about the institution of marriage itself. Resolve to listen and process her thoughts and ideas without being judgmental, making sure she knows how hard marriage can be (especially if she weds an unbeliever). Don't fail to describe how lovely marriage can be with the right person.

Encourage your children to think about questions such as: *Do we share the same values about life, marriage, faith, children and work? Do we believe the same tenants of faith? How important is his/her fam-*

ily? Who will take care of the children if both are working? These are all great questions to discuss prior to settling down with their forever person. Choosing your mate is the third most important question in life. Let's help our kids get it right.

Asking questions that you do not have answers to gives your child (and you) lots of opportunities for reflection. Letting her ruminate over the questions is wise. After those conversations, pray the Holy Spirit invades her heart, mind, and soul with His wise and loving grace and truth. Pray that He will surround her with Jesus-loving and grace-oriented, Holy Spirit followers.

When I was twenty-three, I became engaged to a wonderful man who I had been dating for a while. Although we only dated for a year, we grew up in the same town and went to the same schools. He even took me to a homecoming dance my senior year in high school. The reason I share this part of my story is because I ended up in a broken engagement. One that was difficult for both of us. To be completely honest, there was nothing about my ex-fiancé that was necessarily wrong. He was a kind, generous, successful, and good-looking guy. He loved God. The problem was this—he was not the person God chose for me. In my heart I knew something wasn't right; and because of that, I ended the engagement. I hated hurting him, but I knew it was the right thing to do.

My husband and I dated for almost two years; but we broke up twice before becoming engaged in February 1991. We had a lot of stuff to work out and work through during those years. My husband was a believer. We both had a great work ethic. We had lots of dreams; but when it came to children, he was not sure if he wanted any. This was a big red flag for me. I wrestled with his ambiguity. Children were always in my plan, and I couldn't marry someone who did not feel the same. We obviously worked it out; but I am glad we had that discussion prior to walking down the aisle. These types of conversations with our young adult are a gift.

If you know you've processed the important questions about marriage with your children, it is now time to step back and trust God to do His work. Continue to look and ask the Holy Spirit for more opportune times to speak into their lives. I realize at their age the window of these kinds of discussions for chatting opens and closes frequently. This can be frustrating; but don't stop asking the Father for moments to share grace and truth at His promptings. The Holy Spirit will lead you—just ask.

> If you know you've processed the important questions about marriage with your children, it is now time to step back and trust God to do His work.

💬 SMART REFLECTION

What are the character qualities your young adult is looking for in his future mate? Have you asked him? Who is he intentionally becoming, so that he is the right person for his future spouse?

_____

_____

_____

_____

_____

_____

_____

_____

_____

 ## A NEW POSSIBILITY

What if your young adult allowed you to speak into his life regarding his life mate? What if you asked permission to share your wisdom about marriage, the ups and downs of life, and love?

Father, I believe You have the perfect spouse for my child. I trust You, Lord, to bring them together at Your time and not a moment sooner. Prepare both their hearts for the adventure marriage can be. When they do find each other, I pray they both would know beyond a shadow of a doubt that You have chosen them for each other. And if they are already married, and my child's spouse does not believe or have faith in Jesus, I pray You make Yourself known to him (or her), so they both can enjoy a growing and intimate relationship with You.

TWENTY-FIVE

Purity

For the law was given through Moses;
grace and truth came through Jesus Christ.

—John 1:17

As a young parent, I read books, listened to radio programs, and talked with other parents on the subject of purity—a word which, by the way, doesn't quite say it all. It was a mere substitute for my real concern—sexual intimacy.

Gathering information from select authors and churches, we did our best to communicate proper information to our children. We then challenged and encouraged them to remain pure. That is, *don't have sex*. With the *formula* in place, it was their responsibility to walk it out. In this exchange, however, there was much less talk about purity from a heart, mind, and soul perspective. Sexual intimacy was the central issue.

At puberty, hormones run rampant. To negotiate those hormones isn't easy. Culture responds by saying: live and let live, do what feels good, there are no consequences for your actions, and so on. But in spite of current cultural wisdom, there *are* consequences. Some things are *not* okay and won't be okay outside the sovereignty of God's plan for sexual intimacy. We did our best to give our children a biblical foundation, to teach them that the desire of God is for good and not evil, for benefit, not punishment. Our Heavenly Father is not trying to keep any of us from fun, excitement, or pleasure.

A child can attend Christian schools. They can be homeschooled. They can participate in youth services regularly at church. But that does not mean they are going to understand all there is to know about how to live for Christ with a pure heart. I am convinced the only way they can navigate the temptations and process the lies the world will throw at them is by cultivating a close relationship with Christ on a daily basis. They must seek His mind and heart continually.

Our goal is to trust in the One who can help her in her own spiritual journey. If your child knows Jesus and has accepted Him as Lord and Savior, in one sense she is pure already, cleansed from all sin—past, present, and future. If she has confessed with her mouth that Jesus is Lord and believes in her heart that God raised Him from the dead, she will be saved, and she is therefore, pure and redeemed. God looks at her with eyes of love, compassion, forgiveness, and mercy. He does not see her sins anymore. He sees her as clean, after Jesus shed His blood on her behalf.

As a parent, the questions we must ask are, *Do I believe this for myself? Do I live and demonstrate the life I ask of my child?* Here is another question: *Is it my responsibility to keep my child pure? Can I even do this?*

But ultimately, you cannot control your children or their choices, at least not without creating new and unnecessary complications.

I believe it is *not* our job, nor are we able to keep our kids pure on a myriad of levels. As mentioned above, only God can do that. You can place them in an environment where they will hear about walking in purity—

a church retreat, a Christian school, a youth group, and offer them a plethora of godly books, podcasts, or music. But ultimately, you cannot control your children or their choices, at least not without creating new and unnecessary complications. Jesus, however, *is* able and willing, and desires to love your children and keep them pure until the day of His return. That's good news!

Returning home from a youth weekend that was all about sex, my child said to me, "Mom, I did not realize being pure was more than a sexual thing. It is so much more than that. It is about a pure body, mind, heart, and soul."

I am grateful God taught my child that weekend what purity really means. And what it does not mean.

We are either forgiven and stand before God in this life and the next, covered by the blood of Jesus and His sacrifice for us on the cross, or we are not. If we are in Christ, then we are clean—past, present, and future. Let us teach our children before their teen years about a daily relationship with the Creator of the world. Don't just throw a plan at them for a religious life with its *dos* and *don'ts* or some trendy form of behavior modification. Show your children what it looks like to sit with the Father and seek His face, read His Word, pray His Word daily, and do what Jesus did. With these practices, you will arm your kids for the challenges that lie ahead. When we teach our children that purity is not only about sexual intimacy and all about purity of heart before Jesus, they will be well on their way to understanding a life well lived by the grace and goodness of God.

SMART REFLECTION

What do you believe is your responsibility when it comes to keeping your teenager/young adult morally and physically pure? What are some ways you can help them explore what it means to walk in purity? Will you ask God?

_____

_____

_____

_____

_____

_____

_____

_____

_____

 ## A NEW POSSIBILITY

What if you prayed God would specifically speak to your child's heart about all things pure, lovely, and good? And what if she then came and told you what He taught her?

Father, thank You that I walk in purity every single day, not because of what I do or don't do, but because of what You have done for me on the cross over two thousand years ago. Help my children to understand the same. My heart's desire is to support them through both their good and bad choices and not get stuck there. Thank You that You are transforming my mind through the influence of the Holy Spirit every single day.

TWENTY-SIX

Responsibility

*Each of you must take responsibility for
doing the creative best you can with your own life.*

—GALATIANS 6:5

What types of responsibilities does your teenager/young adult have besides school or participation in an extra-curricular activity? Is he beginning to take responsibility for his world or are you still waking him up for school, making his lunch, and doing his laundry? (Please tell me no.)

With a considerable amount of help from outside sources, I homeschooled my children until the seventh grade. Being at home gave them the opportunity to learn about all kinds of domestic chores like cooking, cleaning, and taking care of themselves. As they became teenagers, busy with sports, friends, and their social life, it became increasingly difficult to pin them down before they ran out the door. They loved the freedom that came with being a young adult, but they did not want to be tied down to their responsibilities at home. A question I asked myself often was, *Am I doing for them what they could definitely do for themselves?*

By the time my teenagers hit their junior/senior year, they took care of

> *Am I doing for them what they could definitely do for themselves?*

most of their own stuff—laundry, waking up on time, completing homework assignments, some cooking, figuring out their own breakfast, cleaning their room, making their bed, and more. You get my point. They were taking personal responsibility for their world, and this was a good thing. Now, there were occasions when they had a lot going on, and they asked me for help. I helped; but I would not allow them to take advantage of me.

As moms and dads, this is a hard transition. We love our kids, and we serve them, care for them, and nurture them for years. To release those responsibilities can be a welcoming experience, but at the same time painful. It signals a new season is coming. God is gracious to slowly open our hand to place something new inside, if we let Him. If motherhood or fatherhood has become a strong part of your identity, and you're feeling a bit lost, I would encourage you to grab a book on empty-nesting, or go and talk with a counselor or coach on how to tiptoe into this next season with joy and excitement. There are purposeful things for you on the other side of all this transition.

There are numerous things you have always done for your children, probably too many to count. But if you keep doing them, you won't be supporting the natural process of growing up. It is a challenging world out there, and it will not serve them well, unless they are prepared with some reality checks. Mom or Dad, step back, so your teen can step up and into their own accountability.

A favorite author of mine has written about the *circle of responsibility* and the *circle of concern*. The circle of responsibility has to do with what we are personally obligated or committed to—an employer, our marriage, our young children, our aging parents, and so on. The circle of concern is something we care about and might worry over or be anxious about, but it is not necessarily ours to take care of or resolve. We may get these two things mixed up. We have good intentions around caring for and caring about people and circumstances, but these two topics are distinct in and of themselves. If a circumstance is within our circle of responsibility, then act. If the situation is within our circle of concern, then pray. Figuring out which circle to be in will bring clarity to the circumstance, relationship, or other matter.

What kinds of questions can we ask ourselves when it comes to our young adults? How will we know whether it is our responsibility or theirs regarding a particular matter? Is it within my circle of responsibility or my circle of concern? Here are a few questions to consider, so you can determine whether to step in or step back.

- *What are your main concerns around the topic?*

- *What feelings does it evoke in you?*

- *What does the Bible say about the topic?*

The problem may be easily solved by sitting with these questions for an extended period of time. I would also consider these questions.

- *What role do I play, or should I play in solving the problem?*

- *How am I to respond?*

- *Is God asking me to act upon the situation or trust Him to intervene?*

Often, when the lines are blurry, we either extend our circle too much, or we don't drawback enough. Either of these actions won't work or prove helpful to anyone involved. Knowing the answers to these important questions will help you keep your sanity, develop your faith in God, and help your children grow up. And after all, this is what we want isn't it?

Smart Reflection

How are you enabling your child toward dependence on you, as they prepare to transition into adulthood?

_____

_____

_____

_____

_____

_____

_____

_____

_____

 ## A New Possibility

Think about a current situation you are dealing with. What if you figured out which circle you needed to be in and acted on it immediately?

Lord, lead me and guide in how much is too much responsibility, and what is not enough. Show me daily what is best for my children, as they mature into the responsible young adults they are becoming. Thank You, God.

TWENTY-SEVEN

Senior High

*Your eyes saw my body even before it was formed. You planned how
many days I would live. You wrote down the number of them in your
book before I had lived through even one of them.*

—PSALM 139:16

How are you coaching your teenager/young adult about the
myriad of decisions she will make, as she gets ready to leave
the nest? In what ways are you being influenced by the world and
what it says about what your child *should* be doing? Are you asking
God, or are you deciding what is best for her?

Giving our children freedom to
choose and express *their* hopes, dreams,
and passions without any kind of
judgment is a gift. Sometimes we
inadvertently put *our* hopes and dreams
ahead of theirs. We assume we know
what is best and what next steps they
should take. Maybe you're following

> Sometimes we
> inadvertently put our
> hopes and dreams ahead
> of theirs. We assume we
> know what is best and
> what next steps they
> should take.

tradition. Maybe you don't like their choices. The important point
is allowing *them* to develop their voice with honesty about what
they want for their future. What is your approach?

I have a childhood friend who did not honor her teenager/
young adult's voice, and the young person ended up on a different

path after his first semester of college. I am not even sure the young adult was ever asked what they wanted to pursue after high school. I believe it was just expected to take a certain path of their choosing. His true affection was pointing him elsewhere toward something his heart was begging him to do. He had known his passion and wanted to pursue it, but his parents wanted him to take a different road. Eventually, his bravery won out, and he is now moving toward that dream with great commitment.

Do you find yourself telling your kids things like, "You can't possibly do that," or "How will you support yourself?" We might also think to ourselves, *What will my friends think of me or them if they make that choice?* But what are their real options, and how will you accept something that might not have been your plan for them?

My daughter and I have had conversations around many topics; and she admits that on occasion, she tells me what she knows I want to hear. These topics include, but are not limited to her future plans, friendships, jobs, or many other things that are important to her. She will readily concede that sometimes it is easier to appear to go along, than to deal with the possible fallout that may occur if she tells me how she truly feels. It kind of breaks my heart.

Our children want to please us. I believe God built them that way for good reason; but not to the point of people-pleasing, where it can grow into a pattern and not serve God, others, or them well.

Ask your children lots of questions and listen without getting your feelings hurt. What an expression of love—to give them a voice to be heard. Giving them a place to speak their deepest dreams and desires will be like sowing seeds into the soil of your relationship that will reap long-term dividends for years to come.

I realize it takes time for young adults to figure out what they want in life. Our tendency is to nudge them toward college or a specific trade. This option is great if that is what they really want. But is it? Do your best to be open and willing to explore all preferences, such as a gap year, vocational training, short-term mission work, an apprenticeship, a dance company, an arts conservatory, or maybe a good old job at the tire store or retail shop.

Making discoveries on their own is much more impactful than us telling our children what to do. They may not conform to what everyone else is doing, and that is okay. When we allow them to explore next steps, we instill in them a confidence, trust, and a deep love and respect for us. Giving them the freedom to choose is like a breath of fresh air.

On the other hand, your child may know their passions and purpose, and pursue them whole-heartedly. Do your best, with the help of the Holy Spirit, to support her in the things God has put in her head and on her heart. Talk it out. Listen attentively. Assist her in a game plan. What a joy to see her full of excitement and life, as she walks into her purposeful future.

Take some time to reflect on how you can encourage your teenager/young adult with a variety of choices. Be inquisitive. Don't respond to everything she says. You know how often she tends to change her mind. They feel strongly about something one day, and the next day she may have new plans. It is an honorable expression of love to take the time to process what she has shared with you.

At a later date, revisit the discussion, but only after you have talked with the Lord. Your child will be grateful for the acknowledgement of her feelings, thoughts, and ideas, which will lead to a trusting relationship both now and in the days to come. As she gets ready to exit your home and graduate high school, you will have given her a voice, trust, and a safe place to land and return to, both relationally and physically. Thank the Lord for the grace given to you to have finished this season of the parenting race well.

💬 SMART REFLECTION

What are some ways you can help fulfill your teenager/young adult's dreams? How can you slow down long enough to listen well and ask God what His plans are for your child?

_____

_____

_____

_____

_____

_____

_____

_____

A NEW POSSIBILITY

What if God opens up a specific time to have a heart-to-heart discussion about what is truly on your teenager/young adult's mind regarding her future? What can you do to make this happen in a creative way? Keep in mind, honoring and trust are key to keep the conversation moving in a positive direction.

Father, help me to be open and listen without judgment to my child's heart. Help me to listen with my two ears, so I can support her, and she can fulfill Your purpose for her life, and not mine. Thank You, God that You are preparing the right moment for this to take place.

TWENTY-EIGHT

Shame

*As scripture says, anyone who believes in Him
will never be put to shame.*

—ROMANS 10:11

Would you recognize the feeling of shame (heaviness, disgrace, vulnerability, humiliation) if you felt it?

- *I'm not good enough.*
- *Why would someone want to hear what I have to say?*
- *I'm humiliated by my child's actions.*
- *I can't go to the lunch, because I feel judged by those women.*

These statements are all shame-based in some way or another. There is a heaviness that comes with guilt and shame. We behave differently. We feel we are less than others, inferior. We feel we are not good enough, smart enough, or worthy enough for certain relationships, either personally or professionally. We don't cut it or hit the mark. We become someone else to cover up the shame, guilt, and pain we are experiencing. It is something we cannot see with our eyes, but we can feel deeply in our soul. Shame

> There is a heaviness that comes with guilt and shame. We behave differently.

is a destroyer. It hurts us, isolates us, and produces nothing good in our lives.

How are you around your teenager/young adult? Is there shame that you have not personally dealt with and now you see it manifesting in your child? Do these look familiar in yourself or your child?

- Isolation

- Depression

- Anxiety

- Anger

- Withdrawal

- Disrespect

Is it possible you have set expectations so high that she is frightened to tell you what is really going on inside of her? Is it possible that she believes you could not handle the truth of her present struggle? Is it possible she feels shame and remorse over choices she has made, so she hides, checks out, or doesn't talk much? Or she just ends up pretending all is well, when in reality, it is not?

When we have the privilege—and it is a privilege—of our children confiding in us about something difficult and we respond in an ungracious way, we damage the relationship and give the enemy a foothold. We affirm the lies of the evil one and push them further away from a relationship with Jesus. They already know they have messed up. Take a moment to love and listen to them intently.

The Lord is not at all surprised with any of our mess ups. Why should He (or us for that matter) be shocked by our child's mess ups? Big or small mistakes, outward sins, or sins of the heart, will not take God by surprise. If you have trained your child up in the Lord, she is very aware of right from wrong and good from evil.

I implore you not to respond negatively when she is courageous enough to open her heart to you about her mistakes. It will go nowhere quickly, and it will not produce what you really want—a life-giving, intimate, and growing relationship with your child. Our children need us more than we think.

Do your best to stay calm. I can assure you that I did not handle every situation with patience. I needed to learn, with the guidance of the Holy Spirit and godly friends who prayed for me. What a joy to have the freedom of candid conversations with your teenager/young adult, as they maneuver around and through the pressures of the world and into adulthood.

I have learned much from my children. I've discovered the decisions my children make as young adults are their decisions. The responsibility in the decision-making lies with them, not me. If they choose differently than I would have chosen, it has no bearing on who I am as a person or as a parent. It is their life, and they can choose as they see fit, even if I don't agree. I am not my children's choices or decisions. I know in my heart that my husband and I have given our children a solid, biblical foundation; and now it's up to them to apply it or not. I have accepted that I will not always approve or even like some of their decisions. But I will always love, support, and be there for them. Hopefully, they will give back to us this same measure of loving acceptance and grace.

When our children walk around with a cloak of shame consciously or unconsciously, it dims their light. You can see it and sense it. The same goes for you. Take off the cloak of shame, and let the grace and guidance of the Holy Spirit set you free.

What if we embraced our kids and loved them through it all? How would that change them, and how would it change you? God is after your heart and the heart of your children. What does He want you to release in your soul and surrender unto Him?

If you find yourself in a place of shame, get quiet and talk to God, just like you talk to a friend. Look up scripture to meditate on and memorize. Have coffee with a close companion, share your heart, and ask them to pray for you. Join a group at church that focuses on freedom. Having done all that, stand, and let your shame go. Take steps toward releasing it forever. Ask God for forgiveness and move on. He has cleansed you completely—past, present, and future. Accept it joyfully. God wants to set you free from the things that hold you back, that limit your potential, and keep you from all that He has for you in this life and the next. This is His desire for your children too. Shame can have no place in your life, if you don't let it.

💬 SMART REFLECTION

In what areas do you struggle with shame? What kind of shame (if any) do you see in your children? How does it manifest itself in you or them? Do you believe your children are evading the truth to cover up choices they have made, knowing they may disappoint you?

_____

_____

_____

_____

_____

_____

_____

A NEW POSSIBILITY

What if you created daily quiet moments to receive words of life, and let them pour over your heart, soul, and mind? Or what if you did this for your children through the spoken word or in a written note? What would that feel like? How would that change them?

Father, I believe. I believe You came to set me free from everything that binds me. I believe You do not want me to walk around with shame. I believe You are for me and not against me. Renew my mind and thoughts, so I can run in the newness of life that You have provided for me. Today, I choose to take off the cloak of shame and put on the robe of righteousness. I will no longer wear what is no longer mine, but will choose all things in Christ.

TWENTY-NINE

Silver Linings

I want you to know, dear ones, what has happened to me has not hindered, but helped my ministry of preaching the gospel, causing it to expand and spread to many people. For now, the elite Roman guards and government officials overseeing my imprisonment have plainly recognized that I am here because of my love for the Anointed One. And what I'm going through has actually caused many believers to become even more courageous in the Lord and to be bold and passionate to preach the Word of God, all because of my chains.

—Philippians 1:12-14

Only with eyes focused on God can we see the silver linings that surface and are revealed through life's difficulties. Have you been in situations or conversations with your teenager or young adult where you have thought to yourself, *What good could possibly come out of this? How is God going to change these circumstances? Will He?*

As I have waded through many conversations with both of my adult children, I have thought these same thoughts. My children have confided in me about a variety of tough predicaments they have faced and inquired about my advice. It is a privilege to be asked. This is our goal, parents. As I coach, advise, and counsel my adult children (with their permission) on what has worked for me

> I do not stay focused only on the problem. I am fully present and listening to connect with them, but I listen to hear indicators of them moving toward becoming responsible adults.

in the past and what God would say, I have paid very close attention to hearing other things in the discussion revealing their character, maturity, and their growth as a person. I do not stay focused only on the problem. I am fully present and listening to connect with them, but I listen to hear indicators of them moving toward becoming responsible adults.

Being aware of this is important. It gives us a moment to pour into them goodness, kindness, love, honor, and respect, in spite of the problem at hand. Bringing these things to light in the midst of a struggle will strengthen who they are, who they are becoming, and who God wants them to be.

I am sure you have offered your opinion and advice without being asked—I have. Our kids need our guidance, but at this point (late teens and young adults), only when requested. The transition from telling them what to do, when to do it, and how to do it, to waiting for them to ask our opinion is a long walk up a steep hill. It hurts. We must develop new muscles of restraint over our thoughts and opinions, if we want to maintain some sense of harmony in the relationship. As we exercise self-control (a fruit of the Spirit), it will allow our children to process their thoughts and come to a conclusion. We may not agree with the outcome; but remember, we were given the privilege to be involved in the discussion. This is not always easy, but very much necessary as parents of burgeoning adults.

In *Empty Nest, Full Life*, Jill Savage says, "Pray, don't say!"

How often do we want to jump in and tell our kids at nineteen or twenty-five, "That is dumb. What are you thinking? You have no money to do that." And so on. Learning to zip it and listen until asked will do wonders for the relationship, both now and in the future. This is what we are after in building a long-term and life-giving relationship with our children. You are not going to get to see the silver linings, if you are not in conversation with them. If you are always offering your advice and opinion without being asked, your kids will not come to you. They will go and ask their friends. Who would you rather they hear from? You or a twenty-something?

Transitioning takes time. It will not be instantaneous. It is a long haul of listening, being quiet, and leaning hard on the Holy Spirit for discernment about when to ask, when to comment, or when to be quiet and let your child figure it out.

I have held my breath (and my tongue) on several occasions with both my children. It is not fun, but it is a must. I can tell you this, the brain learns best through failure. Let them fail. They will learn. You have taught them well leading up to these young adult years. Let what you have taught them have its way in their life. As they see and sense you stepping back and giving them space and time, it will create a new place and new season for your relationship.

Look for the silver linings amid difficulties, challenges, and struggles your young adults face. Calling out the great things you see in them, as they mature will bless them. It will be like blowing wind into their sails. And they will become more confident in moving toward their future. I hope and pray you are headed to a beautiful friendship with your child. What a joy that will be.

💬 SMART REFLECTION

Where have you seen God bring a silver lining out of a difficult or challenging situation? How have you encouraged your young adult along the lines of their maturity and character in handling the situation?

_____

_____

_____

_____

_____

_____

_____

_____

_____

 A NEW POSSIBILITY

What if you listened well and responded with, "Susie, I am confident you will make the right decision in regard to where you are going to live next year." What if you did not give your opinion? What if you let them decide what they think is best, even though you don't think so? How would you feel? How do you think they would feel?

Lord, as my children prepare for this new season of young adulthood, would You lead and guide me in my timing of my opinions and thoughts? Remind me when to ask, "May I give my input?" Transitioning well for both my child and me is so important, and I want to honor You and them in it.

THIRTY

Their Voice

Let each of you look not only to his own interests,
but also to the interests of others.

—PHILIPPIANS 2:4

In what ways are you allowing your teenager/young adult to develop their voice through expressing their opinions, desires, passions, and thoughts? Do you plan intentional time to listen carefully with no agenda? Are you listening to connect or to affirm?

"Listening to connect" versus "listening to affirm" are two different types of listening. "Listening to affirm" is reiterating what someone has said to you. Whereas "listening to connect" is heading into a conversation neutral, without having made up in your mind beforehand how you are going to respond. It also means not having a ready-made story about what you think happened or did not happen and the answer to go along with it. That is not "listening to connect." That is "listening to respond."

But what if you entered the conversation and just listened? What if you asked questions for which you had no answers, and you made no assumptions? How would that feel for you? How do you think it would feel for them?

If we don't "listen to connect," we could end up manipulating, dictating, or controlling the outcome of the conversation. Expressing

Trying to control the outcome of their choices might fit better into your plans, but not necessarily God's.

your hopes and dreams to your children is one thing. Telling them what to do or how to think is quite another. Trying to control the outcome of their choices might fit better into your plans, but not necessarily God's.

It is important to affirm the voice of your kids, as they grow into young adults. It doesn't mean you agree with everything they say. I certainly don't agree with my children on all points. But I often ask myself, *Do they feel like they've been heard?* When you ask yourself the same question, you can answer authentically, after you listened without an agenda, without judgment, and without assumption. When you listen closely for a glimpse into the heart of your child and listen beyond the behavior, the possibility for connection opens up.

There's another important question you will want to ask yourself. Are you hearing what your kids are saying, or are you dismissing their ideas or thoughts because of fear?

Fear is a powerful emotion that can take you in a direction you don't want to go. Are you making up movies in your mind about what you think is going on? We do this as parents, not always consciously, but it happens. I've done it, and I am not proud of it. Pay attention to how you are listening and responding. Be aware of your quick answers, your body language, your facial expressions, your eyes, your words, and your tone.

Consider what is going on inside of *you,* while your child is sharing their opinions or thoughts on an important matter. Sometimes it is not what we say that gets us in trouble, but our body language and facial expressions. Kids can sense your fear, disapproval, and attitude, even if you say nothing.

Both my daughter and son pick up on facial reactions immediately. I can't get away with anything. Had I paid closer attention to a few of these nonverbal cues earlier in my parenting, the outcome of my conversations might have been more influential. My goal is to keep the lines of communication continually open, which is only possible through humility, a tender heart, and guidance by the Holy Spirit.

When my daughter was fifteen, she went through a rough patch. We hit a wall that neither my husband nor I knew how to climb over, and we did not know how to help her. The pain we experienced was hard for all three of us, but more so for my daughter.

We sought the counsel of good friends. We prayed, we cried, and we went to family counseling. She went to counseling, and we did everything we knew to support her, and help her overcome the wall she faced. In the long run, there was much sweetness that came out of the bitter. We learned through practicing, failing, and trying again to hear and be heard. John Maxwell says, "Being heard is like being loved."

As the Lord burned away the old patterns and behaviors in our relationship, a new season emerged between my daughter and me. It was not always easy, but we were worth it. The growth and maturity from that season laid the groundwork for my husband and I to allow her to eventually move to New York City to chase her dreams.

Often in our lives, there is a pruning process that brings about new life, like a necessary ending allowing for a new beginning. As we journeyed through this new season, our hearts were bonded together in a fresh way, stronger and different than in the past. Simple and intentional actions built trust, and a that was worth every pain we ever faced. Our daughter's voice was heard, and she felt loved. Give your teenager/young adult the same gift.

What a difference *truly* hearing can make in your relationship with your kids, but also with everyone in your life. Giving people a voice sets them on the right path in relationships and helps them solidify their identity, as they express who they are and what they believe. In return, you will gain understanding and insight which will support the relationship moving forward. This creates what most of us want—an essence of peace and harmony, especially with those we love.

❞ Smart Reflection

How willing are you to be honest about how well you listen? What changes are you willing to make for the life of the relationship? Will you have the courage to ask for forgiveness if you haven't listened well? Meditate on Proverbs 15:28, "Good people think before they answer. Evil people have a quick reply, but it causes trouble" (GNT).

_____

_____

_____

_____

_____

_____

_____

_____

 ## A New Possibility

What if you heard these words: "Thanks, Mom/Dad. I appreciate your taking the time to really listen and not jump in to give me advice"? What would those words mean to you?

Lord, I pray my heart and mind would be sensitive to Your leading and Your love, as I mentor my child through these transitional years. I'm asking for Your mercy and grace so that my child would know You more intimately because of it. Help me pay attention to the nonverbal cues in both me and my child. And let Your loving grace cover over and always season my words, in both this time, and the years ahead.

FINAL THOUGHTS

Slowing down, thinking differently, dreaming new possibilities, and considering "what if" (positive) situations has been a gift to cherish and share with others. Being a better listener and a much better question asker are skills to be acquired and sought after daily. My hope and prayer is that you are able to apply this new way of thinking and being to your life so that you can cultivate a close, growing, and healthy relationship with your child.

Now to God who is able to give you everything you need: time, space, questions, understanding, peace, joy, answers, forgiveness, freedom, provision, release, and unconditional love be all honor and praise for the grand and gracious things He has done and is doing in all of our lives.

Amen!

ACKNOWLEDGMENTS

There are many friends and family who have helped make this book a reality. My greatest appreciation goes out to those who were closest to me through the penning of this devotional.

Frank: My husband, friend, lover, biggest cheerleader, encourager, and never-giver-upper; I could NOT have done this without your unending support and love. THANK YOU!

Ryan: My fun and determined first-born son who has taught me so much about what to say and not say at the wrong and right times. Your life has helped me to know Jesus better and to put a guard (duck-tape actually) over my mouth. Thank you, Ryan, you are so greatly loved.

Hope: My insightful, discerning, and transparent daughter who has allowed me to fail and fail again. Thank you Hope for ALL of the open, transparent, and honest conversations we've had over the years; without them this book would not have been possible or made as much sense. I love you to the moon and back.

Nanny: My eighty-nine-year-old mom who has always believed in me, no matter what I have chosen to pursue in life. Love you so much, Mom.

Chris: My older brother who has always been an encouragement to me. It was because of the change I saw in him many years ago that led me to my own personal relationship with Jesus Christ. Grateful for our friendship and love Chris.

David: My brilliant writing coach extraordinaire who has pushed me, challenged me, and taught me about the art, craft, and beauty of writing with perspicuity and punch! Thank you, friend.

Regina: My first editor who was patient, honest, and supportive of my writing. Thank you, Regina, for your belief in what could be.

Teena: My insightful coach who has poured words of life over me and into me these past four years. Your words helped me create a world I had no idea was possible. I am forever grateful for your influence and impact on my life, Teena.

And thank you to Saundra, Beth, Janet, Carol, Angie, Amy, Lynda, Debbie, Cheri, Hope, Barbie, and Nancy for allowing me to try out, experiment, pray and talk through the material and design on the pages of this devotional. Your support has meant the world to me. Love you all!

ABOUT THE AUTHOR

Patti Pilkington Reed

Patti Pilkington Reed is first a wife to Frank and mom to Ryan and Hope. She homeschooled her children for approximately seven years with a passion and commitment to impact the spiritual, emotional, and intellectual health, and growth of her children. She is an entrepreneur and owned a Christian advertising business for 18 years in the Dallas–Fort Worth area. Patti's experience includes coaching personal, professional, and leadership development to aspiring entrepreneurs in the skincare industry. Her most recent venture as a new author began over three years ago when she answered God's call to write a devotional book around the topic of parents of teens/young adults.

Patti's passion for parents maintaining a steadfast and life-giving relationship throughout the transitional years into young adulthood is a strong one. Realizing the great need to keep a connection through conversation with our teenagers/young adults motivated her to jump into training and certification in Conversational Intelligence® and eventually became a certified C-IQ coach. She has spent the last 30 years leading, serving, and building people both personally and professionally. Her compassion, creativity, and high capacity encourages others toward action and growth for their own development.

Patti's aspiration for *Face to Face: Smart Conversations with Yourself, Your Teenager, and Your Young Adult* is to create an opportunity for parents to be intentional and courageous through conversation to discover the God-given greatness within each of their children. As a result, a relationship that is enduring, sustaining, and life-giving will emerge.

In her free time, Patti loves reading, shopping, playing word games, and having lunch with friends. Her heart and love for people gives her opportunities to open her home for small group Bible studies, participate in welcoming new visitors, and coaching individuals through the Pastoral Care team at her church. Patti and her husband Frank of *The Frank, Starlene & Hudson Morning Show* (94.9 KLTY Radio) reside in the Dallas–Fort Worth area and have been married for almost 30 years. They have two beautiful adult children, Ryan, who has a career in real estate, and Hope who is pursuing her acting dreams in New York City.

Connect with the Author

patti.pilkingtonreda

reedpatti

pattireed.net

patti@pattireed.net